Vietnam & Beyond

Veteran Reflections

To Mike O'Brien 4th INF

Jim Markson

Jenny La Sala; Jim Markson

Order this book online at www.trafford.com
or email orders@trafford.com

Most Trafford titles are also available at major online book retailers.

© Copyright 2014 Jenny La Sala; Jim Markson.

All rights reserved. No part of this publication may be reproduced, stored in a retrieval system, or transmitted, in any form or by any means, electronic, mechanical, photocopying, recording, or otherwise, without the written prior permission of the author.

Printed in the United States of America.

ISBN: 978-1-4907-4616-6 (sc)
ISBN: 978-1-4907-4615-9 (hc)
ISBN: 978-1-4907-4619-7 (e)

Library of Congress Control Number: 2014916143

Because of the dynamic nature of the Internet, any web addresses or links contained in this book may have changed since publication and may no longer be valid. The views expressed in this work are solely those of the author and do not necessarily reflect the views of the publisher, and the publisher hereby disclaims any responsibility for them.

Any people depicted in stock imagery provided by Thinkstock are models, and such images are being used for illustrative purposes only.
Certain stock imagery © Thinkstock.

Trafford rev. 09/27/2014

 www.trafford.com

North America & international
toll-free: 1 888 232 4444 (USA & Canada)
fax: 812 355 4082

Contents

Dedication		vii
Acknowledgments		ix
Introduction		xi
I	On The Flight to South Vietnam	1
II	Taking Care of Business	14
III	Paperback Writer – The Beatles	36
IV	Who'll Stop the Rain?	54
V	Time is on My Side	67
VI	For What It's Worth	76
VII	He's a Real Nowhere Man	109
VIII	Purple Haze	123
IX	Red Sky in the Morning	139
X	Staying Alive	166
XI	Brothers in Arms	186
XII	The Similarities of War	234
Epilogue		283
Footnotes		291

DEDICATION

I DEDICATE THIS BOOK to my mother and father, Dave and Ann Markson, both whom had intimate knowledge of the consequences of war.

My father was a World War I infantryman who was wounded twice during battle. My mother lost her brother and brother-in-law in World War II. It haunts me to this day that I had no consideration at all for their love for me as I put myself at risk and continued to do so and write home about it during my 366 days "in country" while serving in Vietnam. I am convinced that someone or something was looking out for me. I now know it was them.

I came home without a scratch—or so I thought at the time...

~Jim Markson

Acknowledgments

We wish to thank all of the men and women that participated by sharing their stories in VIETNAM & BEYOND.

It is with tremendous gratitude and pride that we honor each of these men and women for their military service and who were willing to revisit a difficult past. For many, it was an enlightening experience. We hope that it will be the same for you.

~ Jim Markson and Jenny La Sala

Introduction

"Wars damage the civilian society as much as they damage the enemy. Soldiers never get over it."

~Paul Fussell

We all have two people inside of us: One is who we are and one is who we can be. But what if the call to war or any kind of trauma leaves a long-lasting and undetected silent imprint on our souls, interrupting who we could have been?

Wars will continue to come and go, leaving in their wake the lingering effects of the silent weapon called PTSD. Soldiers of yesterday, today, and tomorrow share a common thread of Post-Traumatic Stress Disorder—one that I never realized touched me, my children, or my siblings until after I published my father's wartime letters from World War II as a 101st Airborne paratrooper in *Comes A Soldier's Whisper.*

It must be very difficult for a soldier to return from a group and lifestyle where he served an important military function for his country. A soldier is in charge of others and has a built-in family of peers. He then returns to life back home, where he finds that his family has functioned without him, his kids have kept busy, and his spouse has been handling everything. He is told to find his place back home, yet he closes his eyes and sees a different world and life that he left behind, a life that was surreal in the setting of war, a life of which people cannot even begin to imagine...

VIETNAM and Beyond is a collection of wartime letters written home by Jim Markson from March 1967 to March 1968. James J. Markson was born on July 28, 1947 in Hackensack, New Jersey. He joined the USAF on May 5, 1966 and graduated from Air Police Technical School in 1966. He served four years active duty with Security Police units in New Hampshire, Viet Nam and Holland and was honorably discharged in May 1970.

Jim carried sadness and boxed-up memories from Vietnam, just as my father did from World War II. Perhaps, if it were not for the general divided and oppositional public opinion of the Vietnam War at that time, the soldiers returning home might have been able to open up and begin the healing process. Instead, those soldiers returning from Vietnam were afraid to tell their story. These fears bound each soldier to the other.

We need to explore, question, and understand this silent weapon that follows our soldiers home. I have known three people during my life who have suffered from the after effects of war: my father, David Clinton Tharp, from World War II; my ex-husband, Jim Markson, from Vietnam; and my brother, David Livingston Tharp, from the Gulf War. I have often questioned why angry men surrounded me in my life, their tempers flaring with their sadness evident. Even our children expressed tremendous anger over the years, children of a Vietnam veteran who did not realize that he was suffering from the past. In looking back, I believe now that Jim's PTSD was lying dormant, silently waiting for another traumatic episode before rising to the surface to strike— and strike it did. Jim rarely spoke of his Vietnam service during our 14-year marriage. I was only 20 when he shared with me some horrific things from Vietnam that went far beyond anything I could comprehend. We married in 1972 and were very happy. Our son, Curtis, was born in 1980; our daughter, Holly, arrived in 1983. Little did either of us know that life events would trigger his past and come back to haunt us, both individually and collectively as a family.

VIETNAM and Beyond is Jim's story as told through his letters sent home while in Vietnam from March 1967 to March 1968, along with added reflections decades later. He was in the United States Air Force as a security policeman who provided physical security for Air Force bases in Vietnam. He said that he thought they had it made until January 31, 1968, the opening day of the TET Offensive. Horrific things were happening one right after the other, whereas prior to TET, if just one of those things happened, they would have talked about it for weeks. One morning he woke up. The sun was up and he was still in one piece. He got on a Braniff Airlines 727 that took him out of there. The reception that he received coming back to the United States was pretty poor. It got to the point where, if anybody asked if he had served in Vietnam, he would answer no because he didn't want to hear what would follow if he said yes. He and his fellow returning soldiers kept a low profile by growing their hair long, wearing bell-bottom jeans, and trying their best to camouflage themselves as they transitioned back into civilian life.

Jim had nothing to do with any veterans' organizations. In the late 1990s, a friend approached him as he was walking down the street, saying, "Hey Jimmy, I don't know if you know it or not. You know your friend that was in Vietnam with you in May? Well, he overdosed on heroin and died." In the fall of 2006, another comrade passed away, one who had been stationed with him in Bien Hoa. Jim heard that his friend died, but didn't learn until later in January 2007 that his friend had committed suicide. This began to weigh on Jim, who went to visit the

Veterans Administration. He began counseling in February 2007, attending sessions every week. Jim revealed for the first time things that he never discussed with anyone. His attitude has been that no one ever asked, so they never seemed to care. The counselor discovered that Jim suffered from night terrors that would wake him from a sleep, leaving him out of breath with his heart pounding 90 miles an hour. At times he would break up and start crying. He said that it was like he cracked open a water faucet and began spilling the beans. The mental caseworker assured Jim that this was not something physical, but rather war stress with physical side effects. Jim came from the school of "if it's not broken, don't fix it," so he was always okay a few minutes after waking from his sleep. He never went to see a doctor or asked anybody about it, thinking they were simply nightmares and, when they passed, he let them go. But they never let go of him. The caseworker explained that ignoring what was happening to him was like trying to hold a rubber ball under water. At first, it's easy, but it is always there and constantly pushing and pushing.

Jim was diagnosed with night terrors 39 years after he left Vietnam and 20 years after our divorce. It was a relief for him to finally speak to people about this and share with those who are interested. But at the same time, he was now looking at the other side of the coin. How had it affected the last 39 years of his life? For me, as a Vietnam Veteran's ex-wife and mother of two children whose father suffered from his war experience, I realized that we had all been affected and did not know it.

Could it be that Jim's war related stress affected our son and daughter? Was I as a spouse and caregiver by association taking on my husband's depression and feelings of isolation at the time, thereby creating direct exposure to our children?

We as children, wives, brothers, and sisters also suffer from the effects of second-hand PTSD, contributing to shaping and molding of our personalities, interrupting what and who we could have been. We need to open our hearts and minds to our returning soldiers and help them transition back home again for the benefit of the soldier, his family, and society as a whole.

~Jenny La Sala

"The war in Vietnam is not like these other wars. Yet, finally, war is always the same. It is young men dying in the fullness of their promise. It is trying to kill a man that you do not even know well enough to hate. Therefore, to know war is to know that there is still madness in this world."

~President Lyndon B. Johnson
State of the Union Annual Message to Congress
January 12, 1966

CHAPTER I

On The Flight to South Vietnam

"No event in American history is more misunderstood than the Vietnam War. It was misreported then, and it is misremembered now."

~Richard Nixon, *New York Times,* March 28, 1985

[1]March 8, 1967—Congress authorized $4.5 billion for the war in Vietnam. March 19–21, 1967—President Johnson met with South Vietnam's Prime Minister Ky in Guam and pressured Ky to hold national elections.

---

[1] Vietnam source updates:
http://www.historyplace.com/unitedstates/vietnam/index-1965.html

Saigon
Vietnam

March 17, 1967

Hi Mom,

I got into Saigon yesterday at about 5:00 p.m., Saigon time. I lost track of how long it took us to get here from San Francisco because of all the time changes. One thing's for sure, I did enough flying to last me a long time. We left San Francisco at 12:30 a.m., and from there we went to Honolulu. We stayed there half an hour, and from there we went to Wake Island. Then we went on to Okinawa, stayed there an hour with the next stop at Saigon. That's where I am now. I'll be here for a day or so. I have to wait for a flight to Qui Nhon.

When I got off the plane, it was 93 degrees and real humid. I had a hard time trying to sleep last night because, all night long, jet fighters zoom by all over the place. Out in the distance, you keep hearing explosions like artillery. The food is different. I don't know just what it is either. The water tastes good, but it looks like apple juice. The bread is made from rice and is as hard as a brick.

Right now, I'm just lounging around waiting for a flight. They won't let us go into Saigon, so I guess I'll never really see it. I won't take R&R here, that's for sure. I can't wait to get to my base and get settled and unpack. I don't have both feet on the ground yet.

I never saw so many different kinds of uniforms in my life, with blue berets, black berets, red berets, all sorts of camouflaged uniforms, and all sorts of gadgets and knives. From what I've seen so far, I think I'm going to like it here. But I haven't been here long enough to know for sure.

So long,
Blood & Guts Markson

P.S. As far as I know, this is my address:
A3Markson James J
AF12765694
37th Cmbt. Spt. Cp PACAF
APO San Francisco 96238

Reflections

I received a flurry of letters from my brother and sister, who wrote back scolding me because of the way I signed my first letter home, letters filled with bravado, after General George "Blood & Guts" Patton. Once again I had upset my mother.

After reading my own letters 46 years later, I am astounded at the naivety of my youth. I hadn't even been there for 24 hours and could claim "I think I'm going to like it here."

Upon landing I experienced the first indication that things weren't quite right here. The United States Army Military Police escorted everyone from the plane to a bank teller inside the civilian air terminal. Once at the teller's window, under the scrutiny of the Military Police, we had to empty our pockets of all U.S. currency and change it into military payment certificates (MPC). They even had a paper bill for a nickel! The black market was an avenue for making money. The enemy needed U.S. currency to buy weapons. You could double your money in Vietnamese piastres, change it back to MPC, and

deposit it in your bank account. If you got caught, you were in big trouble—and those who did get caught are probably still in Leavenworth (stateside military prison).

-Jim Markson

Qui Nhon
Vietnam

March 19, 1967

Hi There,

I caught a flight out of Saigon yesterday heading up for Qui Nhon. We got to Qui Nhon about 11:00 p.m. They had no room for us to stay, so we spent the night on cots in the chow hall.

In the morning, I found out that I'm not going to be stationed at Qui Nhon, but at Phu Cat. I showed Mom where it is on the map. It's about 25 miles northwest of Qui Nhon, I think. I got in to Phu Cat yesterday. So far it looks like it's going to be a real nice base when it gets done, but right now they're still building it and things are a mess.

I still haven't done anything yet. I have to process in tomorrow. I can't wait to start work. Just laying around and all this boredom is killing me. There's nothing to do except eat, sleep, and drink. But I'm sure that within the next three weeks, this easy life will come to an abrupt end.

How's everything at home? Is Lucky still healthy as ever? Did Barbara have the other ya ya (baby) yet? I hope everybody is feeling good. I am, except for a small case of the runs that a bottle of Kaopectate quickly took care of.

That's all for now.

So long,
Jim

P.S. There's been a change on my APO number. It is now 96368.

> ### Reflections
>
> The base was "a mess" all right. It was the dry season, and the only thing that was paved was the runway. The entire rest of the base was this reddish dust from the dirt that was everywhere, stirred up from the enormous activity of building a new airbase in Vietnam.
>
> ~Jim Markson

Phu Cat

Vietnam

March 20, 1967

Hi Mom,

Well, I started processing in to the base today, and I'm almost done. I just have to go over to the air police squadron and let them know I'm here.

From what I've heard, I'll have three days training on the M-60 machine gun. Then, most likely, I'll go to work at my regular job once I get all set up. I'm in a hurry to start work, even though I know I'll be doing it for a year. I just can't stand doing nothing all day. At a briefing today, I found out that I can put in for R&R whenever I want. I don't have to wait six months before I'm eligible. Ask Sis if she knows when would be a good part of the year to go to either Hong Kong or Bangkok. I don't know where I want to go for sure. They also told us that, since this base is new, the mail is fouled up. It should take about six or seven days for my mail to get to you. But I don't know how your mail will get to me. The base isn't organized yet.

I'm sending you a couple of samples of the money they use here. The pink one is military money, and it's worth $1.00. The green one is Vietnamese money worth about 8 cents. They call it *piastres*. One thing for sure, I won't even need any money. I'll be making $80.00 a month, and there is nothing—I repeat, nothing—to spend it on except beer and cigarettes. Beer is 15 cents a can, and cigarettes are the same.

The town is off limits except for laundry and haircuts that cost 35 cents. I'm going to get a short haircut. It's too hot and too much bother to comb.

That's all for now.

So long,
Jim

Reflections

R&R means rest and recuperation. The military gave everyone 7 days out of Vietnam for a vacation, all expenses paid except for our spending money. I eventually took my R&R in Taipei, the capital of Taiwan. I went during Christmas. I didn't want to be in Vietnam for Christmas. Upon arriving in Taipei, people from the United Service Organization (USO) contacted me. There was a military family, a United States Marine Corps sergeant, who wanted to have a soldier from Vietnam spend Christmas Day dinner with his family at their home. I had other things I wanted to do on my mind, but I went. The warmth and affection I felt on that Christmas Day bring tears to my eyes even some 40 years later. They had little kids and a Christmas tree. They were from California, and for a brief moment I was "back in the world" (Vietnam jargon for being back in the US). We kept in touch. I was going to visit them in California, but it never happened. It's just one of those things.

-Jim Markson

Phu Cat
Vietnam

March 24, 1967

Hi There,

Well, I finished processing in.

I got all of my equipment. I'm ready to go to work. Yesterday I got issued a brand new M-16 rifle and took it out to the firing range to test fire it and adjust the sights. It will be my rifle for the time I'm here.

I found out yesterday that I'm not staying at Phu Cat. I should be leaving here about the second week in April. They're sending 50 of us back to Tan Son Nhut, which is Saigon Airport and an air base combined. I'm glad I'm going there. That base is fairly old and has a lot more facilities, including a radio station, which they don't have up here. I'll be able to go into Saigon when I get the day off and maybe do some good shopping. In the town here, everything is off limits, except the laundry and the barbershops.

When I get to Tan Son Nhut, I'll send you my new address. That will be the third one so far. I guess it will be a month or so before your mail ever gets to me.

Guess what? The other day I met a guy stationed here in the air police from Garfield, New Jersey. I told him my grandmother lives there. It turned out that he had Uncle Peter as his English teacher. His name is Dominick Librera. He said he thinks he had him from 1962 to 1963. Ask Uncle Pete if he remembers him.

I still haven't been able to unpack my clothes yet. But I'm getting used to it. When I go to Tan Son Nhut, I'm going to try to see Jack Frasso and Richie Spera. They're stationed at Bien Hoa, which is only about 15 miles or so from Tan Son Nhut.

That's all for now.

Jim

Reflections

I would indeed "see Jack Frasso and Richie Spera," friends of mine from Sheepshead Bay, Brooklyn, at Bien Hoa. We hung out at the pool hall. Richie played the bass guitar, and everybody was trying to be like the Beatles. Decades later, both of them would have a profound influence on the course of my life.

-Jim Markson

Phu Cat
Vietnam

March 25, 1967

Dear Mom,

I went to work last night for the first time.

I work the same hours all the time. My hours are from 10 at night to 6 in the morning. I like these hours because there's no sun. It gets pretty cool, even a little cold, at night. I guess that's because I'm in the mountains. There are big mountains all around the base. It's really beautiful country. The only bad thing is all the scroungy towns and villages. They're just like the squatters I saw in Hong Kong.

So far, I like working here. It's a lot better than Pease. I feel that I'm really doing something and that there's a chance something might happen, not like at Pease. Another thing, the people respect the air police for being out there all the time. Everybody helps each other out. There aren't any petty little things that they bother you about. I really think I could get to like it here. But I'll be leaving Phu Cat about April 15 and be sent to Tan Son Nhut in Saigon. I'm still not sure how long I'll stay there—maybe the rest of the year or maybe a couple of months. I really don't care where they send me. The main thing is that I'm used to the living conditions here. That was the hardest thing to adjust to.

Well, that's all for now.
Jim

P.S. Was it a boy or a girl?

Reflections

Vietnam really was and still is "beautiful country." Many years later, in 2010 and again in 2011, I returned to Vietnam. I specifically planned my trips to coincide with the Lunar New Year celebrations known as TET. I wanted to experience this centuries old event as it was meant to be, unlike the carnage that took place during the TET Offensive of 1968.

Pease was the name of the stateside Air Force base that I had been assigned to after basic training, a Strategic Air Command (SAC) base in Portsmouth, New Hampshire. The strictness of a SAC base, coupled with being a security policeman, guarding B-52's on 24-hour alert in below-freezing weather, was the motivation for me to volunteer for Vietnam, which I did. To this day, I don't regret it.

-Jim Markson

CHAPTER II

TAKING CARE OF BUSINESS

"The Vietnam War was arguably the most traumatic experience for the United States in the twentieth century. That is indeed a grim distinction in a span that included two world wars, the assassinations of two presidents and the resignation of another, the Great Depression, the Cold War, racial unrest, and the drug and crime waves."

~Donald M. Goldstein, Introduction, *The Vietnam War*

[2]

April 6, 1967—Quang Tri City was attacked by 2,500 Viet Cong and NVA.

April 14, 1967—Richard M. Nixon visited Saigon and stated that anti-war protests back in the U.S. are "prolonging the war."

---

[2] Vietnam source updates:
http://www.historyplace.com/unitedstates/vietnam/index-1965.html

April 15, 1967—Anti-war demonstrations took place in New York and San Francisco involving nearly 200,000 people. Rev. Martin Luther King declared that the war was undermining President Johnson's Great Society social reform programs: "the pursuit of this widened war has narrowed the promised dimensions of the domestic welfare programs, making the poor white and Negro bear the heaviest burdens both at the front and at home."

April 20, 1967—U.S. bombers targeted Haiphong harbor in North Vietnam for the first time.

April 24–May 11—Hill fights raged at Khe Sanh between U.S. 3rd Marines and the North Vietnamese army, resulting in 940 NVA being killed. American losses included 155 killed and 425 wounded. The isolated air base was located in mountainous terrain, less than 10 miles from North Vietnam near the border of Laos.

April 24, 1967—General Westmoreland condemned anti-war demonstrators, saying they gave the North Vietnamese soldier "hope that he can win politically that which he cannot accomplish militarily." Privately, he had already warned President Johnson that "the war could go on indefinitely."

May 1, 1967—Ellsworth Bunker replaced Henry Cabot Lodge as the U.S. ambassador to South Vietnam.

May 2, 1967—The U.S. was condemned during a mock war crimes tribunal held in Stockholm, organized by British philosopher Bertrand Russell.

Phu Cat
Vietnam

March 31, 1967

Hello There,

I got Sis's letter about three days ago, on the 28th.

Mom, I got your letter today. Tell John and Barbara congratulations! But it's bad news if both of the kids look like the Bissmaiers. I guess Johnny will just have to try again for a Markson.

Sis told me in her letter that you are going to send me the funnies—don't. Instead, when I get settled at Tan Son Nhut, send me the news daily. You can send for a subscription, and they will mail it to me. I should leave for Tan Son Nhut on the 15th of April. Then my mail and everything should start to be straight. Right now, everything is a mess. I still haven't been able to unpack.

I took some clothes to the local laundry. The white underwear and socks came back dirtier than when I brought them in. I'm sure they will have better laundry facilities there. I got paid today. Boy what a nice feeling. We get paid once a month here instead of twice a month like in the States.

Tonight our flight is taking up a collection for a flight party for about 20 or 30 cases of beer and real American hamburgers and barbecued chicken. They need cooks, so I'm going to volunteer my expert barbecuing skills. I'll get relieved off post early to start cooking. The other day, during mail call, we had an alert. A few mortar shells hit right outside the northeast part of the base. They found out in a couple of minutes that the Army—the American Army—shot them by mistake. It's typical. I don't think anybody really knows what's going on here.

That's all for now.

So Long,

Jim

Reflections

"I don't think anybody really knows what's going on here." Reading this sentence 46 years later, I am amazed at the perception skills of a 19-year-old boy who had been "in country" less than a month! It was, to say the least, a very confusing place to be for 19-year-olds, the average age of the American soldier in Vietnam.

-Jim Markson

Phu Cat
Vietnam

April 10, 1967

Mom,

I got your letter today. It took eight days to get here. I'll be leaving Phu Cat on April 15. Where that will take me, I don't know. I've been hearing all kinds of rumors. I won't know where I'm going to stay until I get off the plane. That will mean another address, so the mail still won't be straight for a while.

I've heard that I might go to either Tan Son Nhut or to Pleiku. I don't want to go to Pleiku. It's out in the sticks, just like this base is, so that means the town near it will be just as scroungy as the one here. Tan Son Nhut is right in Saigon. As you know—or if you didn't, you know now—Saigon is an R&R center, so it should be pretty nice. One thing nice about Qui Nhon is that they have a nice beach for military personnel only. Guess what? They have two 16-foot runabouts with 80 horsepower Johnsons on the back of them. They're reserved for officers only. But if I'm lucky, I might just get some water-skiing in before I go to wherever I'm going. I've been taking some pictures, but like I said, this place is scroungy and there's no place to get them developed. Send me to Saigon. I've had enough of this place. In four more days, I'll have been here technically one month. The time seems to be going pretty fast, especially since I'm working from 10 p.m. to 6 a.m. One thing I'm afraid of is that, since I've been here, I just can't get up an appetite. It's so hot and the chow hall has a distinct smell about it that sometimes I don't eat all day. I sure would like to get on the scales. I wouldn't be surprised if I've lost 20 pounds already. I'm sure I'll gain it all back when I go on R&R in Hong Kong. I still remember the steak I had there.

That reminds me. Ask Johnny if he can get in touch with Mr. Pai. I'd like to pay that jewelry shop a visit again. Don't write me anymore until I send you my new address. When you go down to Nassau, how about picking me up some Moustache? Make sure you get the cologne, not the aftershave.

That's all for now.

So long,
Jim

> **Reflections**
>
> Amazing—wanting cologne to wear in Vietnam!
>
> -Jim Markson

Phu Cat
Vietnam

April 11, 1967

Hi,

I got your two packages today, the ones with the travel booklets and the one with the Nestlé Quick and the funnies. Don't send me any milkshakes. The milk over here is some kind of powdered stuff and it tastes terrible. I don't drink it. As far as the funnies go, thanks but when I get settled at Tan Son Nhut, have the news sent to me daily, including Sunday. Thanks for the travel booklets, but don't bother sending any on any place but Hong Kong. I've made up my mind that that's where I'm going, if I go.

Remember I told you they told me I could take R&R whenever I wanted? Well, that's true except the people with the longest time here go first. It should be close to 7 months before I get a chance to go. That should put me right in the heart of the monsoon season. If I go, it would be around February. That's when the rain stops. By then, I'll be so short that I doubt if I'll go at all. I'd be coming home in March.

Well, I hope everybody is feeling fine; I am, except for occasional periods of the runs. I get them at least once a week. I think it's from these C-rations that I eat out on post.

So long,

Jim

P.S. Tell Pop to watch those wise-cracks about what I do with my money. I guess by now you've already found out. The next time you need a loan of $500.00, don't joke because when I send it to you, I'll expect 5% interest on it.

Reflections

I had been in Vietnam less than a month, still a "new guy" with my eyes wide open. I was doing a lot of moving around from one base to another. This was typical of the tremendous amount of activity that became a way of life in the Vietnam that I was to experience. I was 19 years old and had been in the Air Force less than a year. I only had one stripe on my sleeve, A3C, Airman 3rd Class, and yet I had been to Texas for basic training, stationed at a SAC base in Portsmouth, New Hampshire, traveled halfway around the world, and was now headed for my third base in Vietnam. I was part of an enormous entity, with unlimited resources and possibilities limited only by my imagination. Leaving the military after four years, I would never experience anything like it for the rest of my life.

~Jim Markson

Tan Son Nhut
Vietnam

April 20, 1967

Hello again,

Well, I got into Tan Son Nhut on April 15.

After flying all over Vietnam, we finally got to Tan Son Nhut. From Phu Cat, we went to Qui Nhon, and from there to An Khe and then on to Pleiku before stopping at Tan Son Nhut. Yesterday, after being here five days, I found out they have more plans for me. In two days, I go to another base, Bien Hoa. I'll be there for about 30 days. Then I come back to Tan Son Nhut. I should stay at Tan Son Nhut for good when I come back from Bien Hoa. Tan Son Nhut is a real nice base compared to Phu Cat. All the roads are paved, the showers are in the barracks, and they have lockers to unpack in. Although I had to put it together myself, it's still an improvement. They have a snack bar where you can get ice cream, hamburgers, and even pizza pies. They also have an airman's club where you can get beer and all kinds of mixed drinks. This base has a lot better living conditions, but with the better living conditions come the inspections, shined boots, and pressed fatigues. They have these house girls who work in the barracks. You pay them 250 piastres a month and they shine your shoes, make your bed and clean the barracks. The 250 piastres comes to about $2.10 in U.S. currency.

I went into Saigon the other day, and I guess it's just like any Southeast Asian big city. I was only there for about 3 hours, but it's pretty nice compared to Qui Nhon. The only thing is that everybody is out to sell you something and the little kids are always trying to grab something. The standard of living is pretty good. The people are clean looking, and there isn't that stink that you find in the small towns.

Bien Hoa is about 18 miles from Saigon and Tan Son Nhut is about 6 miles away, so it won't be much of a change. I get $1.15 a day extra for going to Bien Hoa. They call it temporary duty pay. I don't mind going at all. Another thing, the last I heard Richie Spera and Jackie Frasso are stationed there as machine gunners on helicopters. I hope to look them up. Well I still don't know my address. I'll let you know soon.

So long,
Jim

Reflections

Tan Son Nhut, Saigon International Airport, was at the time the busiest airport in the world. It was home of Military Assistance Command Vietnam (MACV), often referred to as "The Pentagon East" and was the home of the 7th Air Force. I went from piss tubes to ceramic urinals and toilets that actually flushed. If you couldn't find what you were looking for in Saigon, it wasn't in Vietnam. This was as good as it got. (Eight months later, for me, it was to be as bad as it got.)

My sister worked for Pan American Airlines, and as a high school graduation present in 1965, I was offered my choice of two trips at a discount price from my family. One was to England (the Beatles were very popular), and the other was to Asia—Hong Kong, Tokyo, and Hawaii. The thinking at the moment was to take the Asian trip because it was farther away and more expensive and I would not be able to afford it later on. I took the Asian trip. Ironically, two years later, I went on an all-expense paid "tour" of Southeast Asia courtesy of the Department of Defense.

~Jim Markson

Tan Son Nhut
Vietnam

April 21, 1967

Hi Mom,

When I was at Phu Cat, I took some pictures. Here they are. I'll number them as I go along. The pictures are numbered on the back.

The first one is a picture of the barracks I lived in. Notice the unpaved roads and no latrines or showers. The green bag hanging under the steps is the drinking water. Every time a truck would go by, it would kick up dust that would come and cover everything in the barracks. The second picture is a shot of one of the many bunkers they have all over the base. If you look close, you'll see I got most of my golden locks cut off. It's too hot for long hair. Three is a picture of yours truly and the surrounding countryside right outside of the base. Pretty nice country, isn't it? Sure, but once it gets dark, smart people don't go out there. Number four is another picture of the land surrounding the base with mountains and rice paddies. The fifth one is a picture of the shacks that the country people live in. It's not too good a picture, so you really can't get the idea of just how shabby they really are. Number six is a picture of an old Vietnamese shrine. It's about halfway between Phu Cat and Qui Nhon. Today it is known as Checkpoint Charlie. The shrine is occupied by the Army and the Korean Marines. They use it as an observation post. Number seven is a big picture of Qui Nhon harbor and beach. It's really pretty nice. The mountains have cool air, but the water is warm and filthy. The eighth one is a picture of the beach and the runabouts they have for the officers. I never did get my chance to ski there. I heard that near Saigon they have a place to water-ski. The civilians run it, and you can rent them as you like. Number nine is of me spending a hard day getting a good suntan. Here you can really see my new haircut. And I promise, I'll never cut it short again.

So long,
Jim

P.S. I'm still not sure of my address.

Reflections

Inwardly I was glad about leaving Phu Cat. As a security policeman, we provided physical security for Air Force bases. That meant long and boring hours with guard duty at various posts all around the base. Some of the posts consisted of two-story wooden machine gun towers positioned near the perimeter. The sides of the towers were heavily protected with sandbags; however, the floors of the towers, which had a vertical wooden ladder coming through it for entry and exit, were virtually unprotected. The air base was also brand new, still being built, which meant there really were not any "old guys" to show the new guys the ropes. I vividly remember being driven out in total darkness and being posted on a 2-man machine gun bunker on a hill overlooking railroad tracks. The security policemen that we were relieving handed me a starlight scope and told me the "claymores were over there." I had never seen a starlight scope before, had only heard of claymores watching a John Wayne movie, and neither myself nor the other security policeman I was posted with had any idea as to where we were on the base. To make matters worse, as we got settled with our post, we realized we were in a Vietnamese graveyard. It didn't bother me too much; however, my counterpart, an African American, almost jumped out of his skin and didn't calm down until we were relieved at dawn.

During the shift (10 p.m. to 6 a.m.) we became aware of a K-9 post at the base of the hill, closer to the perimeter fence. This was not a "new guy." Apparently the local Vietnamese liked to "have fun" with the K-9 posts and throw rocks at him and his dog. It was called in to security control, and he was authorized to fire a "warning" shot at the culprits. I was watching everything through the starlight scope and all, but I couldn't see anything along the fence line. The K-9 guy let loose, on full automatic with an entire clip into the air. Whether or not it had any effect, I never found out.

That same night, as it got closer to 6 a.m., I heard noises in the distance. The next thing I knew, I looked through the starlight scope to see Vietnamese people walking along the railroad tracks headed for the base! No one had told me that the civilian workers came to work that way in the morning. Oh well, just another day.

~Jim Markson

Bien Hoa Air Base
Vietnam

April 30, 1967

Hello there,

Well, how was your trip?

I bet I have a better tan than yours. The only thing different is that I didn't get mine under the same conditions. How did Pop like becoming part of the jet set? I hope you had a good time.

Tomorrow is Mayday, and as of today no one can leave the base for the next two days. No one will be off on the next two days also. They're expecting the VC to try to put on a little something for the holiday, so we are not taking any chances.

The VC have been doing so poorly lately that they have to pull something off that's really spectacular because the people are losing their faith in them. Mayday looks like a good opportunity for them.

By the way, did you ever get my money order? I sent it out April 1. How did you like the pictures I sent you? Let me know. Right now, I'm at Bien Hoa air base. I'll be here for about 30 more days. Then I go back to Tan Son Nhut.

That's all for now.

So long,
Jim

Bien Hoa Air Base
Vietnam

May 3, 1967

Hi Mom,

Well, two days ago, I got two letters—one from Johnny and one from Sis. Johnnie's letter was dated April 10, and Sis's was dated March 27. Well, that's the way it goes.

Hey, John, thanks for that cigar, but I won't be able to smoke it. It got all crushed up in the box. No, I'm not in the black market. I'm getting my money from Uncle Sam and nowhere else. You asked me if I needed anything and to let you know. Okay, I could use some pens. Please not Bics or anything like that, but halfway decent ones. Since I've been here, I've lost about three pens that I brought with me. They don't have any here. I don't know where to buy any.

As you know, I'm at Bien Hoa Air Base. I've been here almost two weeks now and I like it here. I'm only supposed to be here for 40 days. But I went to see the First Sergeant yesterday to see if I can stay here permanently. I'm working on day shifts from 6 a.m. to 2 p.m. The duty here is pretty good too, nothing like stateside duty. Nobody bothers you. They have Vietnamese house girls that shine your boots, make your bed, change the linen, wash your clothes, and sweep the barracks, all for about $5.00 a month. I can't complain. The first day I got here I ran into Jackie Frasso. I saw him swimming in the pool. I knew he was here, but I sure didn't expect to see him the first day I got here, especially in a swimming pool. He's been here about 5 or 6 months. He's a crew chief on a helicopter and flies as a machine gunner.

Two nights ago, I had the first bit of excitement since I've been here. At about 3 a.m., the alarm went off, and they called out all the A.P.'s on the base—about 700 of us. Everybody jumped out of bed, threw on their clothes, grabbed their rifles, and ran out to the armory. We were posted and strung out around the whole base.

We were there about two and half hours, but nothing happened. It seems that the K-9 posts spotted some people (they never found out who they were) at both ends of the base, so they sent us out there just in case something was up. Today they had a plane come in that only had one wheel down. It was a Vietnamese pilot in a prop plane. They foamed up the runway, and he made it without a scratch. The only thing that happened to him was when he was getting out of the plane. The fireman sprayed him with foam, and that stuff has an awful smell to it.

Well, that's all for now. Batman just came on television. I can't miss that.

So long,
Jim

Reflections

I learned something on that night back in May 1967 when we were called out and posted all over the base—scared, hot, not knowing what to expect—and I've carried that lesson with me to this very day. It helped me during the Tet Offensive, I was keenly aware of it during 9/11, and as I'm writing this I realize why I keep 3 cases of bottled water "just in case" in my apartment at this very moment. As security police, we never left the base. We were required to have canteens on us, but we never filled them with water. The patrols came by often enough with a cooler of ice water, so why bother? I never forgot how thirsty I was those few scared hours I spent waiting in darkness, rifle in my hands, safety off, for something that never happened.

During the Tet Offensive, the entire security police squadron was called out again on Condition Red (attack is imminent). This time my canteen was full and, without knowing it, I was going to spend the next 2.5 days in a 2-man machine gun bunker, without relief, during what would be known as the Tet Offensive.

On September 11, 2001, I was employed as an operating engineer in a 28-story commercial office building in downtown Manhattan (at 7 Hanover Square), about 7 blocks away from the World Trade Center as the crow flies. I was on the roof and saw with my own eyes the second airliner slam into the South Tower. To quote President Johnson, "To know war is to know that there is still madness in this world." I had witnessed this kind of "madness" before. In a micro-second I was "back," with unexplainable and horrific things happening, rapidly, and a lot of people were getting killed. When I finally got to a phone that worked, I called my son who was living in Brooklyn. I told him to turn on the television, fill up the car with gas, and fill up any empty containers in the house with water. And he did.

It seems like yesterday, a bright, hot, sunny day in South Vietnam. The Air Force part of the base had a swimming pool. The Army guys always made fun of how easy Air Force guys had it. And we did. After all, we even had a swimming pool. And right in front of me was Jackie Frasso, a friend from Sheepshead Bay, New York. I couldn't believe it, and neither could he! He was having a lot of fun with some other Army guys from his unit, enjoying the pool. We spoke and promised to meet up as soon as both of us had some free time. A wallflower he was not. Jackie was one of the more colorful guys from the neighborhood, always into and up to all sorts of things. He was little older than me, and here now in Vietnam, a door gunner/crew chief on a UH-1 B Huey. I was in awe.

~Jim Markson

CHAPTER III

PAPERBACK WRITER
~The Beatles

> "Vietnam was the first war ever fought without any censorship. Without censorship, things can get terribly confused in the public mind."
>
> ~William Westmoreland, *Time* magazine, April 5, 1982

[3] May 9, 1967—Robert W. Komer, a former CIA analyst, was appointed by President Johnson as deputy commander of MACV to form a new agency called Civil Operations and Revolutionary Development Support (CORDS) to pacify the population of South Vietnam. Nearly 60 percent of rural villages in South Vietnam were under Viet Cong control at the time, and CORDS distributed $850 million in food, medical supplies, machinery, and numerous other household items to the population in order

---

[3] Vietnam source updates:
http://www.historyplace.com/unitedstates/vietnam/index-1965.html

to regain their loyalty in the struggle for the "hearts and minds" of common villagers. CORDS also trained local militias to protect their villages from the Viet Cong.

May 18–26, 1967—U.S. and South Vietnamese troops entered the Demilitarized Zone for the first time and engaged in a series of fire fights with NVA. Both sides suffered heavy losses.

June 1967—The Mobile Riverine Force became operational, utilizing U.S. Navy Swift Boats combined with Army troop support to halt Viet Cong usage of inland waterways in the Mekong Delta.

Bien Hoa Air Base
Vietnam

May 12, 1967

Hi Mom,

Well, I'm sure you've heard or read by now that mortars and rockets hit Bien Hoa.

I don't know how many people were hurt, but I'm fine. It will take more than some skinny little VC to get to the son of a World War I veteran. Last night was some experience. I hope it doesn't happen again in a hurry. I had just gotten into bed at about 12:45 a.m. I came in late because I was supposed to have the day off. I was throwing the bull over at Jackie Frasso's barracks. The first shell hit at about 1:00 a.m. I ran into a bunker. It was the fastest move I've made in years. At about 1:30 a.m., all of the A.P.'s got called out and posted along the perimeters. There were a few VC trying to get on base, but nothing much happened. I was up all night and had to work the day shift. I finally got to sleep around 4:00 p.m. this afternoon.

Ever since the attack, rumors have been flying all over the base. If it's in the papers, how about cutting out the articles and sending them to me? Then I can know for sure just what damage they did. It seems funny that I have to write home to find out what happened here.

I've been getting letters from mom from the 4th and the 7th and one written April 10. Boy, that mail is fast. I think it's just about straight now. That picture you sent me is pretty good. The ya ya has that greedy grin on his mug there with that cake in front of him. You wanted to know if I ran into Underwood. He came over here on the same plane with me. We've been working the same hours ever since we got here. Two more days and I scratch off two months. I haven't tried that Kool-Aid yet, but I'll let you know how it is. The other day, I ran into George Rosales. He's at Tan Son Nhut waiting for a flight to his base. He's not going to his original base. He's going to some small outfit. I don't even know how to spell it.

So you don't like being a part of the jet set? I guess some people don't know what good is. As of now, I consider myself a well-seasoned traveler. But all of my traveling bills are paid for. I even get 6 cents a mile for moving from one base to another. I went into Saigon last Saturday with Rosales. There sure are a lot of stores there selling all kinds of things. Most of the stores were closed. I guess Saturdays must be some kind of day off for the Vietnamese.

Well, that's about all the war stories I have for now. I bet you thought I forgot, didn't you? Well enclosed is a $10.00 money order. Happy Mother's Day!

So long,
Jim

Reflections

May 12, 1967—I remember it well. It was my first time experiencing a mortar and rocket attack. Throughout the barracks area were bunkers/shelters that you were to go into in the event of a mortar/rocket attack. And this is what we did. Although they were poorly constructed (55 gallon drums filled with cement and a metal roof heavily covered with sandbags), they did give us more protection than being in the barracks. Luckily, there was not a direct hit on a bunker filled with GIs. It could have been devastating. We could hear explosions in the distance and then the unmistakable white flash and loud "crack" of a direct hit on a nearby air police barracks. It was empty and up until a few days earlier had been my barracks. The guys who lived in it walked around for days in their underwear and flip-flops until they could scrounge up clothes and uniforms; everything they owned was destroyed. Once it became obvious that the rocket attack was over, someone inside the bunker yelled out, "If there are any air police in here, they better get going." Oh, damn, yeah, that's me. By the book, rocket and mortar attacks were usually a prelude to ground attacks. Out I went, got my boots on, reported to the armory, and was posted until relieved. Once again the adrenaline was flowing. There was no ground attack. I find it amusing that early on in my tour I was asking my family to send me news about an attack that I was personally involved in halfway around the world. It was just another day. There was no critique, no debriefing, only rumors as to what had happened the night before. This lack of information would become epidemic months later during the TET Offensive in Saigon.

I'm glad to read that I remembered Mother's Day.

-Jim Markson

Bien Hoa Air Base
Vietnam

May 24, 1967

Hello Sis,

I got back to Tan Son Nhut today and again unpacked and got ready to start work again.

I sure didn't want to leave Bien Hoa. Frasso and me were having a real good time. Yesterday, my last day at Bien Hoa, I finally got my chance to fly in a helicopter. It was Frasso's ship, *The Widow Maker*. It was great. Even though it was a non-combat mission, it sure sounded good when the pilot called into the tower for clearance. We were "Mustang Five" to operations saying, "This is Mustang Five preparing for takeoff with Pilot Gawkoski, Co-pilot Frasso, Crew Chief Delano, and Gunner Markson." The captain let Frasso fly from Bien Hoa to Saigon, but he wouldn't let him land it. There were too many helicopters flying around the port. We had to go to Saigon to have the front gun fixed. We were there about two hours when they told us they couldn't fix it today.

We took off again when we got a call from the tower: "Mustang Five, you just dropped your left rocket pod." The rockets on the left side of the helicopter fell off just as we took off. A lot of people came running out, but they [the rockets] can't go off unless they are fired. I took a couple of pictures of me next to the helicopter and one while we were over Saigon. Then I ran out of film.

If I get a chance to get stationed back at Bien Hoa, I'll be able to go up every day that I have off. I also took some pictures of that hut that was hit during the attack. By the way, it was an air police barracks where my flight [crew] slept. I didn't sleep there and was about 3 huts away. I just can't get off the helicopter kick.

I can't wait to go on a regular mission. The helicopter that Frasso flies is a gunship. It's pretty well loaded with weapons. It has 14 rockets, a gun up front that shoots grenades at the rate of 250 per minute, and two M-60 machine guns on each side. The doors are wide open and you sit out on the side of the ship with a safety belt attached to you. What gets me is when you make a sharp turn and go all the way over on one side and nothing falls out the door. I guess it's the momentum of the turn that keeps you inside.

I was told today by the operations sergeant that there is a slim chance I can go back to Bien Hoa and to come and see him in a week. I will do that. I'm going to put the film in tomorrow. You should have it in about a week or so. Don't get excited about me being in that picture of the hut. I was either at work or asleep when all the newsmen came. Bien Hoa is about 15 miles from Saigon. I received your brownies a few days ago. They were pretty fresh. I still have a few hidden away. Oh yeah, Sis, I'll go half on that light you're getting for Johnny. Have you seen the jacket I sent to the little ya ya? I figure it will be just what he needs for the jetty this summer. I hope it's the right size. Send me a picture of him in it, will you? What size does he wear anyway? Listen, could you let me know some good name brand watches? Is Lucien Piccard a good watch? I want to know what to look for when I go on R&R. I've heard that Australia will become an R&R port starting in July. If it does, that's where I'm going. I was looking at some material for suits the other day. That H. Lee suit made in Hong Kong has offices here. They cost $57.00 for the best material they have, custom made any way you want it. They have hundreds of colors. I'm going to get a few made up.

Well, that's all the war stories for now.

So long,
Jimmy

Reflections

Indeed, we were "having a real good time." It was surreal, to put it mildly. Here we were, two friends who really hadn't known each other too long. I had met Jackie casually from hanging out on Sheepshead Bay Road, the pool hall, and the Shore Café (a local neighborhood bar). Suddenly, propelled by current events 12,000 miles away, we found ourselves involved in a war. We would get together in the early evening, sometimes go into town, Bien Hoa, and eat out. Jackie had been in country longer than I. He showed me around. I listened in awe at the stories he and his fellow "Mustangs" would share about their daily missions. Alcohol and marijuana were easily available and would enhance the story telling. On one occasion, the topic of discussion was how many ribbons we would be able to wear on our uniform when we returned stateside. You were awarded the Vietnam Service Medal after spending 30 consecutive days in Vietnam; the Republic of Vietnam Campaign Medal was awarded after 6 months in Vietnam. I wanted a whole chest full of medals. I had bragging rights on my mind. Jackie mentioned that if I flew one mission in his gunship I would be eligible for the Air Medal: "All you have to do is fly one mission over hostile territory." I asked, "When are you over hostile territory?" Jackie quickly replied, "As soon as you take off." The plan was hatched. I wanted an Air Medal. One small problem, I was in the Air Force and had no business flying as a door gunner in an Army gunship. No problem:

"You know how to shoot an M-60?"
"Yep."
"Show up in a uniform without any markings and I'll get you on."
And he did. I will never forget the events of that day. I can replay them in my mind as if they were happening right now.

While reading my own letters 47 years later, I can't help thinking about what my mother felt as she read them. As a young woman she lost her brother and brother-in-law in World War II. Both my mother and her sister Margaret, a war widow who re-married, named their sons after Uncle Joe. My middle name is Joseph. Recently I came across letters from World War II. My Uncle Joe, an officer in the infantry, had been wounded in Germany. My grandmother, born in Czechoslovakia, wrote him a letter—"Joey, you always looking for trouble, now you find it"—lovingly scolding him for getting hurt. A few months later, Joe was killed advancing on a small town in Germany. Why is it we "look for trouble"? I can almost hear my mother saying, "Jesus, Mary, and Joseph, Jimmy why don't you just stay on the air base where you belong?"

I never did get stationed back at Bien Hoa, and that was the one and only time I flew as a door gunner. Also, it was impossible for me to put in for the Air Medal because what I did could have gotten me into trouble. And yes, we broke rules. The mindset was "What are you going to do to me? Send me to Vietnam?"

-Jim Markson

Tan Son Nhut
Vietnam

May 26, 1967

Hi Mom,

Well, yesterday I worked my first shift at Tan Son Nhut.

I'm working nights from 8:00 p.m. to 4:00 a.m. After working day shifts at Bien Hoa, I don't like midnight shifts anymore. I sure hope I don't stay here. This base is too big and too much like stateside duty. They have open locker inspections twice a week. Mainly they're just looking to see if you're collecting any war trophies like hand grenades, pistols, etc. They may be right. But I don't like the idea of any kind of inspections. I'll find out if I can go back to Bien Hoa next week.

I got paid $32.00 extra today for my stay at Bien Hoa. It's TDY pay. It's a dollar a day for having to move away from your home base. I think I'm going to buy myself a watch with it. I broke my other one. I twisted the knob that you wind it with, and it came off. Have you ever heard of Seiko watches? I hear they're supposed to be pretty good and pretty cheap.

I ran out of film the other day. When I went to the BX, I found out they don't carry my kind of film. Could you send me a couple of rolls of color C-126 film? Thanks.

I've been reading the world temperatures and I see that it's warming up in NYC. It looks like it won't be long before you break out the water-skis. Oops! I mean, if I remember correctly, buy a new set of water-skis. I haven't been able to buy any here yet, but you never can tell.

So long,
Jimmy

Tan Son Nhut
Vietnam

May 28, 1967

Hi Mom,

Here are some more pictures on the spot, where the action is, pictures from your roving reporter, Jim Markson—or should I say Flash Markson?

As I did before, I'll number them on the back and tell you what they are about. Number 1 is a picture of old Blood & Guts Markson, all decked out in my war suit. I bet you're having a hard time seeing me with my camouflaged fatigues on. I doubt you've ever seen one before, but anyway, that's an M-16 rifle that I'm holding. Number 2 is one of me standing next to Frasso's helicopter. See the name written on the front gun, "The Widow Maker"? Number 3 is a full-size picture of the ship. To my right a little above the runners is one of the rocket pods. We dropped the one on the other side all over the field by accident when we took off. But they didn't go off. Number 4 was taken out the door of the helicopter. It's Saigon from the air. Too bad it was a cloudy day. Number 5 is a picture of the A.P. hut that got hit by that rocket at Bien Hoa. Number 6 is one of the huts next door to the one that got hit. Number 8 is another shot of the hut, and number 9 is a picture of the guys who lived in the hut trying to find some of their clothes and stuff that was burned in the fire. Well enough of that.

Yesterday I went into Saigon and had shrimp cocktail and yes, a filet mignon, which cost me $2.50 for both. I've heard rumors that the steaks in Saigon are made from water buffalo and monkey. After eating that so-called filet mignon, I don't doubt it.

It wasn't too bad though, but not what I'm used to. I did a little shopping. I saw something for Johnny that I'm sure he will be able to use when he graduates college. I'll send it in the mail first chance I get. You can expect it in about 2 weeks.

Well, that's about it for now, except I can't wait to know if I'm going to be able to get back to Bien Hoa. I think I'm addicted to helicopters.

So long,
Jimmy

Reflections

It was just another day in my Vietnam. I sent home some pictures. What I've found out from reading *Comes a Soldier's Whisper* is that when David Tharp is writing home about things that start to get to be about being wounded and getting hurt and possibly killed, he and I both used almost identical words to change the subject. David Tharp: "Well, enough about that." My letter: "Well enough of that." Another similarity is that both of us dated our letters incorrectly. My mother would correct the dates as she received the letters home. David's misdating of a few letters would be caught by a reader of his book and was later corrected with the explanation that he continued writing 1944 when it was actually 1945. The wars change, yet the soldiers in them seem to be eternal. They are identical in their hopes, fears, and beliefs in what they are doing and who they are doing it for, with a willingness to risk their lives and take chances, if need be.

-Jim Markson

Tan Son Nhut
Vietnam

June 5, 1967

Hi there,

Mom, here is $100.00 money order. Cash it and take $50.00 out that I owe you and put the other $50.00 in my bankbook.

Jimmy

P.S. Now that I have a box number for my mail, how about having the news sent to me? Look on the editorial page. I think it has the prices up on top. Make sure I get the 7 days a week one.

Tan Son Nhut
Vietnam

June 5, 1967

Hi Pop,

Well here it is, June 5 already.

I'm knocking down my third month. Time sure is going pretty fast. I got two letters from you the other day. You didn't put the APO number on the address. If I were you, Pop, I wouldn't do too much loafing around all day. You better find something to keep you busy. Look what happened to Uncle Peter after just loafing around. I hope he comes out okay, Aunt Helen too. Speaking of Aunt Helen, I haven't seen her or any of the Milans since Johnny's wedding.

I'm glad you liked that jacket I sent for Drew. It should be good out on the jetty. Sis told me he got his first boat ride last week and really likes it. Now that I know that Drew likes boats, I don't have to worry about not having a boat for next summer when I come home.

I also received some letters from Mrs. Shanahan. She sends me newspaper clippings and stuff from *Reader's Digest* and religious stuff. I appreciate the thought behind it, but if I wanted to read *Reader's Digest*, I'd buy it. I never was a holy roller, and I'm not going to start now. So I would appreciate it more if she would stop sending me anything. Things like that bring me down. You have no idea how easy I have it here. I'm stationed just about in the middle of Saigon, and it may as well be Times Square. Another thing, all the big brass is here in Saigon, so the BX has just about everything. In fact, Tan Son Nhut is almost just like a stateside base. I even feel a little guilty when I collect that combat pay. I go to Saigon and eat filet mignons. I found a place to water-ski, but the water is dirtier than Gerritson Creek, so I'm not going. You call that a war zone? I don't. I can really say I'm having a pretty good time here. So don't worry too much about me. That's the main reason why I'm going to try to get out of Tan Son Nhut. I feel wasted here and, with Saigon so close, it's going to be hard to save money like I would like to.

Well, I hope everybody feels fine at home. Let me know when drew starts skiing, and Pop, I don't want to hear any more about you loafing around.

So long,
Jim

P.S. See you in about 9 months and 10 days

Reflections

Like everyone stationed in Vietnam, we all knew exactly how many days we had left to do. I was no different. And yes I was feeling guilty about how "easy" I had it. Saigon was and still is an amazing metropolis, especially for a 19-year-old. I had been based at two other air bases that had many fewer amenities; the guilt came because I was always aware that the war really was real. I had daily reminders of the seriousness of where I was.

As a security policeman, we controlled all movement throughout the airport. Gates and checkpoints were everywhere. We stopped all vehicles except the "meat wagon," a sinister, dull, flat black painted truck, with wooden sides covered with a loose-fitting canvas that would kind of spookily flap as it went by. It was like something from Ichabod Crane's Headless Horseman. It had no markings and kept its flashers on, day and night. Out of respect, no one stopped this vehicle. It got the priority it deserved. It carried the dead from the flight line to the mortuary, also located at Saigon Airport. Day and night, C-7 Caribous, C-123 Providers and C-130 Hercules cargo planes would come and go from Saigon. We knew that, as the ramp, opened there was always a possibility the cargo would be body bags from the field. I could not take my eyes off of them, with their boots sticking out of the bags in positions a living person's feet would not be in. Often the bodies had decayed and started to smell. The meat wagon always smelled, which was another reason not to stop it at the gate. Knowing what the smell was from would make me dry heave at times.

The mortuary was close by the security police compound. There was a small bridge to cross over whenever we went in or out of the area. This bridge went over the "Red River," so named because of the color of the water in the drainage ditch, made that way by the blood drained at the mortuary. There was a constant to and from cadence of those shiny aluminum caskets that were used for transportation stateside, just like the ones you see today arriving at Dover, Delaware.

The mortuary had a wooden, horizontally built, privacy fence around it. I'll never forget as a "new guy" at the Nhut, I took the bait. Walking with other SPs, someone asked, "Hey, Markson, you ever see what's on the other side?" Eagerly, and showing no fear, I climbed up to where I could see over the fence. Instantly, I knew I had been set up. I can see it as if I am looking at it right now: a bright sunny day, 6 to 8 bodies of American soldiers without any clothes on, lying on the concrete, being hosed off by South Vietnamese workers. I never looked over that fence again. To this day, I don't have to.

I was assigned to Charlie Sector. We worked nights, and most of what I call "My Vietnam" always took place at night, in darkness, interrupted by the red orange glow of the flares dropped by "Spooky" that would eerily light up the evening as they oscillated on the way down in parachutes. In the distance we could see air bursts, artillery rounds exploding at tree-top level. They were so far out that we could see them, but only hear a muffled *whooomp* at best. On occasion we even got to see and hear "Puff the Magic Dragon" do its thing. The first time I witnessed it, it sounded like some prehistoric monster delivering a fluid neon line of bullets out of the darkness.

The war was always "out there" somewhere. This was Saigon, so the war wasn't allowed to get close and I never really felt threatened. After all, those were the rules. One day, with very little notice, those rules would change.

~Jim Markson

CHAPTER IV

WHO'LL STOP THE RAIN?
~Creedence Clearwater

"North Vietnam cannot defeat or humiliate the United States. Only Americans can do that."

~Richard Nixon, speech, November 3, 1969

[4]

July 1967—General Westmoreland requested an additional 200,000 reinforcements for the 475,000 soldiers already scheduled to be sent to Vietnam, which would bring the U.S. total in Vietnam to 675,000. President Johnson agreed to only an extra 45,000.

July 7, 1967—North Vietnam's Politburo decided to launch a widespread offensive against South Vietnam. Conceived in three phases, the first phase involved attacks against remote

---

[4] Vietnam source updates:
http://www.historyplace.com/unitedstates/vietnam/index-1965.html

border areas in an effort to lure American troops away from South Vietnam's cities. The second phase (TET Offensive) was an attack against the cities themselves by Viet Cong forces aided by NVA troops, in the hope of igniting a general uprising to overthrow the government of South Vietnam. The third phase involved the actual invasion of South Vietnam by NVA troops coming from North Vietnam.

Tan Son Nhut
Vietnam

June 10, 1967

Hi,

Mom, I received your letter dated June 5 today.

Things are the same over here, nothing new. Yesterday, I went to Bien Hoa to see Frasso and the First Sergeant to see if I could get back to Bien Hoa permanently. He told me to see the colonel, the squadron commander. When I went to see him, he had already left for the day. So I'll have to go down there on my next day off. I get every Friday off. I stayed at Bien Hoa, sitting around drinking with Frasso. He had to fly this morning at about 5:00 a.m. I got up at about 3:00 a.m. and caught a helicopter ride back to Tan Son Nhut. Boy, do I like helicopters. My chance will come soon.

I got Sis's care package the other day. Thanks for the film, peanuts, sour balls, and flashbulbs. Thanks, but I don't need any more flashbulbs. I still have the ones that I brought over here with me. As far as sending me more packages with stuff, how about some more brownies for a start? Then, how about some Ritz crackers and some cheese spread in an aerosol can? It's the kind that comes in the same thing as whipped cream. Do you know what I mean?

Uncle Bill finally got some class, huh? It's about time somebody started buying something they don't really need. I'm sure you put in your usual, "You don't really need that, do you?" Well, I may like T-Birds, but when I come home I'm going to get a corvette if it kills me.

I don't know what makes you think I'm growing a beard. I'm not. Well, I've got to go to work now.

So long,
Jimmy

June 21, 1967
Tan Son Nhut
Vietnam

Hello there,

I was looking at the world temperatures, and I see that NYC has been having hotter weather than Saigon. I bet it's nice boating weather.

I'm sorry to hear about Uncle Pete. I didn't think he would go so fast. How old was he?

I know that this month is Father's Day and your anniversary, but I'm low on money and can't send a gift. So Happy Father's Day and Happy Anniversary. I'll see what I can do on payday.

I got the picture of Drew. He looks a lot different from the last time I saw him. He's losing that dumb innocent look. Now he looks like he knows what he's doing.

I was out on post the other night, as usual, when the sergeant came around checking posts. I told him I wanted to go to another base. He asked why I didn't like it here. I told him I was tired of sitting on bunkers all night. So he said, "Oh, you want some action. I'll fix you up with some tomorrow night." So now, instead of sitting on bunkers, I fill sandbags and build bunkers. He thought he was pretty slick, but I'd rather be doing something than just sitting around. I'll build bunkers for the next 265 days. I don't care. Today is my 100th day in Vietnam. Getting short.

I got a letter from Johnny Lund the other day. He's on a Caribbean cruise now.

So long,
Jimmy

Reflections

I caught on to traveling by helicopter. All I had to do was go over to the heliport and listen to the almost never-ending destinations of the helicopters that were leaving Saigon and hop on. I flew back and forth and would spend the night at Bien Hoa and hang out with Jackie. Sometimes I'd grab my camera and just hop on a huey without caring where they were going. That was a mistake. I vividly remember once landing at a small outpost in the middle of nowhere and learning that there might not be any other hueys coming or going until dawn. Luckily there was. It was not the kind of place I would have liked to spend the night.

It was stupid to ask the non-commissioned officers (NCO), a special and very clever breed, any questions. His remedy, having me fill sandbags, is classic military. And I deserved it. With 100 days in country, I was beginning to get the feel of the place and get cocky.

The term "short" was Vietnam jargon for having fewer days left to go on your tour, normally 365 days. I would realize later on that I was going to spend 366 days for my tour. February 1968 was a leap year and we were all keenly aware we could get hurt or killed on our first day as well as our last. That extra day was a long one. A few weeks before I went home, I was on duty when VC gunners got lucky. A rocket scored a direct hit on the civilian air terminal, where men were only hours away from getting on a "Freedom Bird" that would take them back to "the world." Some went home in a casket instead; others were wounded. It could and did happen. Rocket attacks were random, deadly, and demoralizing, and the Viet Cong used them as best they could.

As we counted down our days, we called it "getting short." Once we had fewer than 100 days, we became a "short timer." The term had another meaning in downtown Saigon, with the ever-present sea of pimps and ladies of the evening trying to make a buck. The sales pitch came in two varieties: a woman for overnight was a "long time" whereas a quickie was a "short time." The term had duality.

-Jim Markson

Tan Son Nhut
Vietnam

June 27, 1967

Hi Mom,

I got both packages the other day with the crackers, cheese, and brownies.

They were fresh and came in handy. The cheese was just what I wanted. Johnnie's graduation present is on the way. It should be there in a few days. I think it's an appropriate gift.

How about you? Sis told me that they're going to build some low-rent housing projects on Emmons Avenue. Are you really going to move? If you do, make sure you let me know. I don't want to come home on leave and not know where I live.

Well, that's it for now.

So long,
Jimmy

Tan Son Nhut
Vietnam

July 2, 1967

Hi there,

Well, there's another month gone. Time sure is flying by. I just can't wait until July and August are over.

It bothers me to know that back home you are having the same weather that I'm having here. I can't help thinking of the boat and water-skiing every time it's real hot and there's no wind. But when the winter comes, I'll be glad I'm here. I haven't been able to do any skiing here and I don't think I will in the future either.

Did Johnny get my gift yet? What do you think of it? Right now I'm trying to get myself a VC uniform, the black pajamas that they wear. If I get it, I'll take a picture of myself in it and send it home. Don't be surprised if you get a pair of black pajamas in the mail.

That's too bad about Uncle Pete and his will and all. I guess he never thought he would go. Well, neither did anybody else, and just when his son, Jackie, was trying to make friends again.

If I remember right, you bought me a bottle of Moustache cologne when you were down in the islands. How about sending it to me? Thanks.

So, I'm a hero already, with my name on the plaque in front of the Bill Brown Post. I'll have to see it when I come home for sure, just like in the movies. Wow.

Well, that's about it for now. Keep me posted.

So long,
Jimmy

Tan Son Nhut
Vietnam

July 3, 1967

Hi there,

Here's another money order that brings my account up to $150.00.

I sure would like to have a thousand saved by the time I come home, but I think my R&R will put a dent in my savings. Well, that's life.

I forgot to tell you about the newspapers. Don't have the newspapers sent to me from the news. Instead, could you mail me just the complete Sunday edition? Thanks.

That's all for now.

So long,
Jimmy

Reflections

The days were starting to add up. I wasn't moving from base to base, and care packages and items that I requested from home were arriving pretty regularly. Life was good. There was some kind of an order, and some things actually made sense. I was homesick and missing the water-skiing season back home. I was buying custom-made souvenirs n downtown Saigon—black Viet Cong pajamas even.

My father was a World War I veteran, infantry, wounded twice. He had a kind of a small crease in his forehead from a piece of German shrapnel. He was born in 1901. I was from a second marriage, making him 46 years older than me. The age difference was unlike that with other boys I grew up with, but I was unaware of it. He always held military service in high regard and at one time was the commander of the local American Legion, Bill Brown Post. When I was a young boy, the Legion's Memorial Day parades were quite the scene. This was the mid-1950s, and World War II veterans would fill the streets in formation and march to different locations where there were plaques on the wall with the names of local servicemen and women who had served and some who had died in wars and in service to their country. I must have been around 10 years old and didn't really understand what it was all about, however I knew it was big and serious too. At each memorial, uniformed men would fire rifles in a solemn ceremony of respect for the names on the plaques. We would scramble for the shell casings as they were ejected out of the rifles and place the empty shells in between our fingers and make them into whistles.

As a past post commander, my father must have made arrangements to have my name added to a plaque outside the Bill Brown Post. As it turns out, I don't recall ever visiting the plaque and although I presently live only a few blocks from where it was, the post is no longer in existence.

It took me about 30 years before I had anything to do with a veteran-related organization. In response to a mailing, I finally joined the Vietnam Veterans of America.

In my day-to-day activities I meet contemporary Vietnam veterans, and from the conversations that ensue I tend to believe that the trauma resulting from the way we were treated as we arrived home—the ridicule, disdain, and humiliation—was equal to or worse than what we experienced during the war. And without any instructions or a manual of any kind, we reacted.

I like to relate it to other groups in respect to "hiding." As Vietnam veterans, we "hid"—grew our hair long, wore bellbottoms and love beads, and I even grew a beard. We kept our mouths shut and tried our best to fit in with whatever part of society we could. I can recall times when I was asked if I had been in Vietnam and I would just say no. It would eat me up inside that I had chosen to answer as I did. For 25 to 30 years we hid instead of coming out of the closet; we came out of the bunker when attitudes finally changed. In 2011, I—as my father before me—became a commander of a veteran organization, VFW Post 107, one of the oldest VFW's in the United States, started by World War I veterans. As a group, we weathered those years with a dignity comparable to none other. We owe it to all those who never came home and to the thousands who did come home and are no longer with us to tell the story.

As I write this, I have never been prouder than I am right now to have been part of the Vietnam experience.

-Jim Markson

Tan Son Nhut
Vietnam

July 13, 1967

Hi Mom,

Well, it looks like the monsoon season has finally got here. It rains every day, off and on. But when it rains, it rains real hard.

Right now, I'm just getting over a nice cold. It was a real winner. I didn't get the brownies and Moustache cologne yet. I haven't been able to check mail today. I'll go down in a little while to see if they came in yet.

I received two birthday cards, one from Drew and the other from the Markson family. Thanks.

I'm glad Johnny liked the smoking jacket, but don't ask me how to tie it. A friend of mine showed me, but I couldn't put it in writing.

You seem concerned that I might get tired of brownies. Well, I can't think of anything else in the way of food. Maybe you have some suggestions. Right now though, I need a volunteer. Who would like to volunteer and send me $20.00? I ran short early in the month. I either misplaced or lost some money and $20.00 would come in real handy. I could use it ASAP. If you send it, send it in the form of a money order. Thanks.

I got a letter from old Kevin. He told me that he's working as a trainee in the 60th precinct down on Coney Island. Kevin is going to be a cop? Will wonders never cease?

I saw that picture of Johnny is his graduation suit. Boy does he ever look like a boob. You'll never see me in an outfit like that.

Tomorrow marks my fourth month over here. Time's not going so fast anymore. That's because I don't like Tan Son Nhut. It's a little too much like a stateside base.

So long,
Jimmy

CHAPTER V

TIME IS ON MY SIDE
~The Rolling Stones

"I don't know where I'm going, but I'm on my way."

~Carl Sagan

[5]

July 29, 1967—A fire resulting from a punctured fuel tank killed 134 U.S. crewmen aboard the *USS Forestall* in the Gulf of Tonkin in the worst naval accident since World War II.

---

[5] Vietnam source updates:
http://www.historyplace.com/unitedstates/vietnam/index-1965.html

Tan Son Nhut
Vietnam

July 16, 1967

Hi Pop,

Yesterday—I mean Friday, my day off—I went to Bien Hoa to see Frasso.

Of course, I went via helicopter. While I was there I went over to the air police squadron to see some of the guys I used to work with. It seems like they're expecting a big attack there very soon.

They're using all sorts of stepped-up security measures, and they've issued weapons to everyone on base, including cooks, truck drivers—everybody. During the night I heard all sorts of explosions from our artillery firing out into the jungle. It's very loud and sounds a lot like the rockets that hit the base last May, so I didn't get much sleep. It was my night off, so it didn't matter much anyway.

I still didn't get those care packages. I hope they didn't get lost. About that phone call you plan on putting through on my birthday, I think you'd better cancel it. I don't know how they would get in touch with me, and you're not sure about the time change. Things would be pretty well messed up. I can call you from here, but I'm not too sure how it works. I think it would be better that way. I'll check it out in the near future and let you know what's up.

That's all for now.

So long,
Jimmy

Tan Son Nhut
Vietnam

July 21, 1967

Hello Pop,

Thanks a lot for the $20 and double thanks for that extra 10 spot.

It sure came in handy, Pop. They say that old soldiers never die, they just fade away, but I can be sure of one old soldier that is still coming on strong. Thanks again, Dad.

I got the newspaper the other day. You can't imagine how good it was to read it, even though I got it about 10 days old. I wonder if it would be too much trouble for you to send it to me every day. I hope not.

I got a letter from Johnny. It seems like he really is moving up in the bank. I'll start looking around for a movie projector as soon as I get a chance. Congratulations to Pat Milan. I hope the kid is feeling okay. Where did Uncle Peter ever save up so much money? Too bad he didn't make up a will.

Sis sent me a couple of pictures of all of you, Drew too, the ones where you are all dressed up. You sure look good. Drew seems a little bigger too. I imagine he'll be a lot different in 8 more—oops, 7 months and about 3 weeks.

The other day I got a 3-day pass and went to Bien Hoa. I was supposed to fly as a machine gunner on Frasso's helicopter. Everything was all set for me to fly until the day I got there. Some officer started blowing his top and wouldn't let an outsider from the Air Force fly with the Army. Boy was I disappointed. Anyway, I got a ride in one and took a bunch of pictures. I'll send them as soon as I get them developed.

So long,
Jimmy

Tan Son Nhut
Vietnam

July 26, 1967

Hi there,

Well things are pretty dull around here, for me anyway.

I wish I could go to another base, anywhere, just to break the monotony. Last week, they came around asking for volunteers to go to Vung Tau. It is about 50 miles south of here. But I couldn't go because I wasn't the right rank, maybe next time. I have some pictures to send you. Right now they're being developed. I'll send them out when I can. Most of them, in fact all except one, are taken from a helicopter ride from Bien Hoa to Saigon.

About my birthday, I'd rather have you deposit the money in my bank account back home. If you send it to me, I'll just blow it. Thanks. Could you ask Sis if she would send me a small Zippo lighter, like the one she has with the parachute on it? They have lighters over here, but they're all big ones and don't work well at all. I brought one with me, but it got all banged up and doesn't work anymore.

I got a letter from Kevin's cousin, Billy Golding. He's over here too. He's up north of here, about 300 miles away. He said he's supposed to be moving to Bien Hoa in September, so I should be able to look him up. It's pretty lousy up where he is, a place called Chu-Lai. He had to build his own barracks before they had a roof over their heads. He'll probably really appreciate the good living when he comes to Bien Hoa. It's two different worlds, northern South Vietnam and southern South Vietnam.

That's it for now.

So long,
Jimmy

Tan Son Nhut
Vietnam

July 28, 1967

Hi,

Well, today is my birthday. Those golden days of being a teenager are gone.

I'm 20 years old, 20 years old. What's Peter Pan going to think of me now? I promised him I'd never get old. I feel like an old man.

I went to a few BX's today and looked around for the cameras and projectors that Johnny sent me a list of. I found one movie camera that he had priced at $139.00. They want $95.75 for it here. I'll send him the pamphlet of just which one it was. They don't seem to have any Bell & Howell projectors, but they do have Argos projectors. How good are they? They may be getting Bell & Howells in, but you never can tell what they will have in stock from week to week.

I got a letter today from Lt. Pat Sovich. She's in Guam. From her letter, I can't tell if she likes it or not. But she's counting the months, so I guess it's not too good. From what I've heard about Guam, I'd rather be here than there.

I got another package in the mail today but I can't tell what it is cause the mailroom was closed and I couldn't get it out. I will let you know what it was in the future.

Hey, listen, if I don't write all the time, don't get upset. Lately, I don't have much to write about and working the hours that I do doesn't give me too much time. I'll keep you posted as often as I can.

So long,
Jimmy

Reflections

Time was going by relatively slowly for me. I felt that I had to write home just to keep my family, especially my mother, happy. I was running out of money. Saigon was a very interesting place, and there were plenty of Vietnamese nationals eager to separate you from your cash. The monsoon season was approaching. I can remember clearly asking Jackie, who had lived through a monsoon already, what it was like. "It's like the ocean falling out of the sky." Yep, that's what it was like, all right. To this day I rarely use an umbrella. I don't own one. I'll wear a baseball type hat similar to what I wore in Vietnam, but that's it. The rain came down so hard the streets would flood and you were going to get drenched no matter what you did, so why fight it? Inwardly, nowadays, I kind of chuckle to myself when I see people scurrying around at the beginning of a rain shower, racing for cover as if their lives depended on it. I know for a fact—and I learned this in Vietnam also—that no matter how wet you get, you will eventually dry off.

It's just another one of those things that I never think about. I just do it. Yet when examined as I am privileged to do by reading my own letter 47 years later, the roots are easy to follow.

I always enjoyed getting the newspapers from home, no matter how many days old they were. I guess it gave me a connection of being where I wished that I had been: home. When I've sent care packages, recently to the troops in Iraq or Afghanistan, I try to squeeze in a copy of the local paper like *The Bay News* or *Our News* or *Newsday*, just something that they used to read to give them the imaginary moment of being there and to remind them that home is really still there, waiting for their return.

I turned 20 years old while I was in Vietnam. I was no longer a teenager. And as the days and experiences yet to come would occur, along with my youth, I would also lose my naivety and my blind trust in authority and things I just took for granted. For the rest of my life, I would and I've seen it on bumper stickers, "Question Authority".

-Jim Markson

Tan Son Nhut
Vietnam

August 1, 1967

Hi,

Well, here are some pictures for you.

I took them from a helicopter on the way from Bien Hoa to Tan Son Nhut. Some of the pictures have spots on them. I think they're from the developing process that they use over here. How do you like the one of me in my off-duty uniform? I just had to try it on in picture number 1. The pictures numbered 2 through 5 give you an idea of the rice paddies and the muddy canals that are all over the place. Picture 6 is one of the types of living conditions outside any of the cities here. This is on the outskirts of Saigon. Number 7 is a part of Saigon. The whole city is congested, but not all of it is as bad as the picture looks. The rest of them are just pictures of the country and the Saigon River. I'll try and get some more pictures of Saigon from the ground next time.

Well, the night of my birthday, the VC was working out just outside our base. They hit 3 bases with rockets and mortars. The bases were only 12 miles from here, and I could see the flashes and hear the explosions during the whole attack from my barracks. One of the towers on our base spotted the VCs rocket positions and directed artillery and helicopters in on them. The VC was 7 miles out from here, and their rockets have a range of 10–12 miles. Why they didn't hit Tan Son Nhut, I don't know.

I don't know if I forgot to tell you or you didn't get my letter, but I got the Moustache cologne and brownies. They came in a little late, two days ago. I got the crackers and cheese. Thanks. As of today, August 1, another month is gone. Time can't go fast enough.

So long,
Jimmy

Tan Son Nhut
Vietnam

August 6, 1967

Hi Mom,

Well, things here at Tan Son Nhut have been pretty quiet lately, but nearby it's been a different story.

As I told you in my last letter, the VC hit 3 bases within range of Tan Son Nhut. About 3 nights ago, they hit an Army depot about 6 miles out of Saigon with mortars and blew up a fuel storage area. Just like last time, I could see the explosions in the sky. It lit up the sky a bright red color. The fire lasted about 4 hours before they could put it out.

Enclosed is the clipping of the camera for Johnny. I don't know how much it would cost to send home, but if I send it by ship instead of air, it might take a little longer and be a lot cheaper.

I got the two newspapers you sent me on August 3. Were those the ones you sent by airlift? I think I got the others a little sooner.

I am running a little low on clothes. I'm wondering if you could send me two Banlon short-sleeve shirts, medium size, in blue and green along with a pair of black Levi's. I take a 30" waist and 31" length. You can get both shirts and pants in the Army & Navy stores. Make sure the pants are Levi's.

So long,
Jimmy

P.S. Do you show the pictures to Kevin when he stops over?

CHAPTER VI

FOR WHAT IT'S WORTH
~ Buffalo Springfield

> "This war in Vietnam is, I believe, a war for civilization. Certainly it is not a war of our seeking. It is a war thrust upon us and we cannot yield to tyranny."
>
> ~Francis Cardinal Spellman, speech, 1966

August 9, 1967—The Senate Armed Services Committee began closed-door hearings concerning the influence of civilian advisors on military planning. During the hearings, Defense Secretary McNamara testified that the extensive and costly U.S. bombing campaign in Vietnam was failing to impact North Vietnam's war-making ability in South Vietnam and that nothing short of "the virtual annihilation of North Vietnam and its people" through bombing would ever succeed.[6]

---

[6] Vietnam source updates:
http://www.historyplace.com/unitedstates/vietnam/index-1965.html

August 18, 1967—California Governor Ronald Reagan said the U.S. should get out of Vietnam, citing the difficulties of winning a war when "too many qualified targets have been put off limits to bombing."

August 21, 1967—The Chinese shot down two U.S. fighter bombers that accidentally crossed their border during air raids in North Vietnam along the Chinese border.

Tan Son Nhut
Vietnam

August 8, 1967

Hi,

I got your package of brownies yesterday on the 7th.

They were the freshest and best baked batch that I've gotten so far, not too well done and just perfect. Thanks.

I also received the newspapers of the 23rd, 26th, and 27th. I got them on August 6. It took pretty long this time. I think it would be better if you just sent me the Sunday editions instead of every day, okay? I'm sure I told you before, but since you keep asking me, yes, I got the Moustache cologne and brownies a couple of weeks ago. Tell Sis that I went to look for Russ Morey today out at the airport. It seems he must work in town. I'll try to find him there.

So long,
Jimmy

Tan Son Nhut
Vietnam

August 11, 1967

Hi Sis,

I knew you would like that picture of me in Johnnie's smoking jacket. That's my off-duty uniform. I have some more pictures that I'll put in to be developed. You ought to get them in about a week or so.

That picture you sent me of some baby-faced soldier isn't me, but it did look a little like me. Thanks for that lottery ticket. When do they have the drawings for the winners?

I went to see Russ Morey yesterday. He told me of a hotel, The Majestic. I went there and checked it out. It's a pretty nice hotel, right on the riverfront. He didn't seem to remember you at first. I thought you were his secretary but he told me that when you worked for him, he had 700 people working for him. When you get here, he'll be on vacation in the States. He told me he's over here for 2 years. I don't remember how long he's been here already. He's got a real nice office and a Vietnamese secretary that speaks perfect English. That's pretty rare.

I'm running low on handkerchiefs. The laundry always manages to lose a few on me every time I bring them some. I could use about 10 or so. Thanks.

So long,
Jimmy

P.S. Don't put any insignia on my lighter

Tan Son Nhut
Vietnam

August 14, 1967

Hi There,

As of today, I'm over 5, with over 5 months in Vietnam with only 7 more to go.

I got a letter from Sis two days ago, and I see my desperate attempt to prevent you from putting an insignia on my lighter proved futile. I already know what I want on the lighter and I'm sure you can't get it stateside. What did you put on it? Send it to me anyway. I can still use it. But if there's anything on there that a "Lifer" might have, I'll have to ask you to send me another one. Thanks for that starfish. I'm trying to figure out a way I can put it on my helmet.

As far as "do I like the things you are sending me," yeah. But your prophecy came true. I'm getting tired of brownies and cheese and crackers. I can't think of anything else offhand. How about some of Grandma's chicken soup? Maybe you could send me some oatmeal cookies, if you think they won't get stale. But if you can't wrap them up good, don't send them.

Yes, they really do have Batman over here. I've seen it a few times. The Vietnamese go crazy over Batman.

I can get a movie projector over here, no sweat. The only trouble is that I can't get a good one. They only have Argus, not Bell & Howell. I'll see if I maybe I can borrow one.

That's all for now.

So long,
Jimmy

Tan Son Nhut
Vietnam

August 20, 1967

Well, hello there,

Here are some more pictures.

I think they're pretty good. The first one is of me in my war suit. The second one is a close-up. Notice the hat. It's called a "go to hell" hat. They call it that because it has no shape at all and is sort of a sign of rebellion against the lifers. Just like the hoods back home wear long hair. Over here, you wear a "go to hell" hat.

Up at Phu Cat and Bien Hoa, you could wear them. But at Tan Son Nhut, there's too much brass around. The third and fourth is a picture of "The Group." That's Rosales on the left. He was from my last base. "The Group" are the guys I usually hang around with. The fifth one is on the way into Saigon. Rosales jumped out at a stoplight and took the pictures in case you were wondering how I got the picture. That's a motorized cyclo that I'm in. See those yellow roofed, blue-bodied cars? Those are the taxicabs. They're just a little bigger than a Volkswagen.

Hey, did you hear about Jeane Dixon's prediction? Well, she's got some good ones out now. She said that Tan Son Nhut will be overrun and blood will flow out of the main gate at Bien Hoa and cause WWIII. First we hear about this prediction, and then we get an intelligence report of a VC battalion with orders to zap Tan Son Nhut. According to Jeane Dixon, all of this is supposed to happen by the elections, which are sometime in September.

So long,
Jimmy

Reflections

I found myself living out quite an adventure. I also had time off and did my best to get around and keep my family at home abreast of where I was and what I was doing by sending home pictures and as much info about them as I could. I was also very aware of things the enemy was up to. I remember clearly that evening the Viet Cong rocket crews hit Bien Hoa airbase. Located about 18 miles northeast of Saigon, we watched the flashes light up the sky and heard the explosions from our barracks. We expected to be called out, but it didn't happen. Having been stationed recently at Bien Hoa, watching the rocket assault had a more of a personal meaning to me, as I knew people who were there. Subconsciously, all of my senses were on high alert. Although we kind of had a feeling that we were lucky that it was them and not us who were getting hit, I was ready to bolt to the nearest bunker at the first sign of a rocket landing on Tan Son Nhut. Over time, the reddish orange glow of the nighttime sky became commonplace. During the TET Offensive, Saigon burned for weeks. It was another reminder that, even though I was stationed in Saigon, a secure area, the enemy was very real, close by, and resourceful. There was never a shortage of rumors. I don't recall Jeane Dixon's predictions. I even tried finding them recently on the Internet without any success.

Thank goodness I finally received the cologne! What a whiner.

There was an American civilian who my sister had known who was working in Saigon. I tried looking him up and I found him. My sister worked for Pan American Airlines and was trying to come visit me for 3 days. And she did indeed get to visit, stay at the 5-star Majestic Hotel, built by the French. The 377th Security Police brass even gave me and another security policeman a 3-day pass so we could show her around! Scout's honor, I am not making this up. I even took her out to the heliport at Tan Son Nhut and got her on a chopper ride. The crews were more than willing to give a "round eye" (Vietnam War nomenclature for a non-Asian woman) a ride on their ship.

My letters are starting to mirror my dislike of the "Lifers," a derogatory term for members of the Armed Forces who were staying in for 20 years, making it their career, as in a sentence of 20 years to life. Since I felt that I had been lied to by my recruiter about becoming an air traffic controller which resulted in me becoming a security policeman, I developed a growing contempt for the Air Force and everything about it.

And yes, Armed Forces network TV showed Batman. The Vietnamese kids loved it, and I had my family send me some T-shirts with the Batman logo on it.

-Jim Markson

Tan Son Nhut
Vietnam

August 22, 1967

Hi Sis,

This article about a Vietnamese family in Saigon made me laugh. I like the part that I have in parentheses. As far as hearing the "rat-tat-tat" of VC machine guns on the fringe of the city, it's rare, very rare. However, if you were here last night, you would have heard it. They caught 3 VC with a mortar less than a mile off base and there was a lot of shooting. But most of it was the U.S., not the VC That part about the *whoosh* of 140 MM rockets? Never happens… The only time they were ever used in South Vietnam was at Bien Hoa, 18 miles away, and Phu Hoi, 12 miles away.

I'm sure you must have enjoyed reading the article. You will hear artillery and air strikes during the night, on and off all night long. I don't know if they'll keep you awake or not. I don't remember if they kept me awake, as I'm used to it now. I just found out that the monsoon won't be over in October because it started late. So bring an umbrella and raincoat, if you plan on staying dry.

I found out there's a guy in the squadron who has a small 8-millimeter movie projector. I haven't asked him if I could borrow it yet. But I'm pretty sure he will, unless he wants to send it back home. So bring those films.

Thanks for the magazine on those cars, but I doubt if I'll be able to save enough money for one. Here's the negative of that picture you wanted. By the way, what happened to my cigarette lighter?

So long,
Jimmy

Reflections

This letter, written to my sister must be about her upcoming visit to Vietnam. Obviously she sent me an article out of a newspaper about what it's like living in Saigon. She probably was (and rightfully so) a little frightened about spending 3 days in a war zone. I'm sardonically amused at the naivety of my youth as I read my words: "the *whoosh* of 140 mm rockets? Never happens." I was so smug and confident in American superiority that Saigon was a safe area and that rockets were just not allowed here. These people were, after all, called gooks, slopes, dinks, and zipperheads—they were no match for us. And not once, not even remotely, did the thought that one day we might lose this war ever enter my mind.

"Never happens" was a commonly used term by the Vietnamese, as in "Never happen, GI," especially when we were negotiating the price of some goods or services downtown. The 140 mm must have been from the news article. The rocket of choice, and as far as I know still used today, was the Russian-made 122 millimeter rocket.

My sister did indeed make good on her plan for a visit. Roger Underwood and I showed her around. There was a curfew at night, and all security police had to spend the night on base. My sister's hotel room had a balcony that looked out over the Saigon River and beyond. After nightfall she had a ringside seat to the war, out in the distance, gunships patrolling the city, artillery air bursts, and flares being dropped by spooky. She didn't like it, and I can't blame her, it's just that's the way it was. And I did get to borrow the movie camera and film her visit. I have it on a CD and can reminisce at will. After 3 days she got on a plane and safely made it back to the world.

-Jim Markson

Tan Son Nhut
Vietnam

August 25, 1967

Hi Mom,

I received the pants and two shirts today.

It seems like I've been gaining some weight. That 30-inch waist seems a little tight. But they usually loosen up after you wear them. They are just the way I want them. The shirts are fine too. I don't remember how I stand with my clothes back home. But do I have any cotton button-down collar, short-sleeve shirts? If I do, please advise this station of how many and the color. Hey, Mom, do you remember how you used to cut down a pair of tan Levi dungarees and make them into a bathing suit for me? I could use another one. But before you send me one, let me know if you remember just how and where to cut them.

Well, Saigon will be put off limits from September 2 through September 4. These are the days of the Vietnamese elections, and there's usually a lot of fun and games down in town, like riots, bombings, and all that good stuff. Guess I'll miss it. I would have liked to get some pictures of the fun, but that's the way it goes.

I saw that picture of Librera. I see him around every once in a while. He works law enforcement on day shifts. I work security on the midnight shifts, so we don't run into each other much.

Tell Sis that Diamond Jim will treat her to the hotel room. If I know Sis, she is in her usual state of financial chaos, so the room is on me. As far as getting a brochure on the hotel, you don't need one. Believe me, it's the number one hotel. But don't expect the "Mandarin." I've changed my mind again about my R&R. This time it's permanent. I'm going to Taipei and that's final. Could Sis send me a couple of travel folders on it, please? Just send a few, not a thousand, just one or two good ones.

I like the peanuts and fruit juice you sent me. But I've found that supermarket that Sis wrote me about. It's in the Cholon section of Saigon, and they have Hawaiian punch, peanuts, beans, and tuna fish, so you don't have to send me any. The only thing I can't get are home-cooked things and the stuff I write you for. You could send me some lobster tails or filet mignons anytime! Or, if you can't manage that, I'll settle for some sand cake.

Not much happening around here. I'm off tonight. So I guess I'll go chase a couple of blondes.

So long,
Jimmy

Reflections

Getting fat in a war zone! Like I said before, Air Force guys had it easy. It's just the way it was, especially being stationed at Tan Son Nhut and being so close to Saigon. I'm even asking my mother for a custom-made bathing suit! And being picky about it too! Good grief, I know a few infantry guys who would really feel sorry for me.

I was getting ready for my sister's visit, and even went so far as to pay for her hotel room. Even as a one striper, Airman 3rd Class, I made a lot of money because of the exchange rate. Compared to the average Vietnamese we were wealthy guys. My sister worked for the airlines and loved to travel—still does. If there was any place on the planet that you were thinking of visiting, just a mention to my sister and she would have all the info and then some in no time at all. She even knew where the supermarket in Saigon was! But you couldn't get sand cake there though. My mother was an excellent baker, and sand cake was just one of my favorites.

"Chase a couple of blondes"—that was a phrase my father would say when he would see me sitting around the house with nothing to do. He'd kid around and ask the same question: "Well, why don't you go out and chase a couple of blondes tonight?" There were no "blondes" in Saigon, so I thought I'd kid around with him so he would know I was thinking of him.

I'll never forget the day I left for Vietnam. I had been on leave for a few weeks and it was show time. My mother was very attentive, making sure I had everything or anything for that matter that I needed. She was serious, but not upsetting. My father, however, was very busy with some kind of plumbing project with a neighbor, under the kitchen sink. I mean, I was all dressed in my Air Force blues, ready to go out the door, and he was not doing or saying anything except working in the kitchen. I looked at my mother and shrugged my shoulders, then nodded my head toward my father. She said something to him and he came over to me, but couldn't look me in the eye. He shook my hand, started crying, and looked away. I had never—and I mean never—seen anything like this from my father. So then I was headed out the door with my head spinning, and for the first time, I was getting scared. The plan was for me to drive my sister's brand new Plymouth Satellite out to Kennedy Airport, where she and my brother would meet me and see me off. I was on my way out to the airport, upset about my dad, and they played Buffalo Springfield's "For What it's Worth" on the radio. I got even more upset as thoughts of "what the hell am I getting myself into" raced through my mind. I met my brother and sister as planned and that went well. I checked my bags and was waiting, so I decided to call home. My father got on and he was in tears, being very apologetic and saying all kinds of things that I really can't remember other than I was getting more and more worried about what lay ahead. I got on the plane headed for San Francisco. The drinking age at the time was 21, and the stewardess asked me if I would like a drink. I told her a scotch and soda. She asked if I was 21, and I said no. She asked if I was going to Vietnam, and when I said, "yes", she said, "I'll get you one."

It's too late now, Jimmy. As the song goes, "Well it's one, two, three, what are we fighting for, don't know and I don't give a damn, next stop is Vietnam."

-Jim Markson

Feel Like I'm Fixing To Die
And it's one, two, three, what are we fighting for
don't ask me I don't give a damn, next stop is Vietnam
And it's five, six, seven, open up the pearly gates
ain't no time to wonder why, whoopee we're all gonna die
-Country Joe McDonald song excerpt

The frigid flight line

Even the barracks were cold...

The flight line was no joke, KC135's & B-52's, each B-52 had 4 nuclear weapons. Thank God they never launched.

Sandbag Bunkers outside of our barracks,
Phu Cat Airbase March 1967

Brand new barracks at Phu Cat Airbase March 1967

Security Police Barracks destroyed in rocket attack, Bien Hoa Airbase May 22, 1967. There were no casualties. Everyone was already in a bunker

Guys I hung out with

Saigon suburbs from a helicopter

I sent this home to my brother, had to try it on first!

Picture from a helicopter

Hamming it up with Robert Uchman from New Jersey

Squatting like The Vietnamese with a guy
named Zhiem on my right and Ralph

Me and Roger Underwood, Roger would help
me escort my sister around Saigon

Yep, Yours Truly, water skiing the Saigon
River, in country R & R Center

I even had the nerve to ski slalom!

Me and Carey Bradley, somewhere downtown Saigon

Street traffic downtown Saigon, hasn't changed much

View of the Saigon River from the balcony of The Majestic Hotel where my sister stayed

The Presidential Palace, now known as The Unification Palace

Taken from a helicopter somewhere over Vietnam

My friend Johnny Lund, USMC somewhere in Vietnam

Me & Pete, a Filipino friend & aircraft mechanic who worked for Air America & helped show my sister around

Me & Peter lighting up in a Saigon River tour boat with my sister

In the sticks, outside the entrance to the In Country R & R Center

Looks like Ham and Lima beans (barf) on a midnight shift on the bunker

Inside the bunker I would spend the TET Offensive in with an M-60 machine gun

"Security Control, we're seeing white flashes from the post opposite the civilian air terminal" "Markson, you see any white flashes out there"? "Oh, no Sarge, we didn't see anything". Flash bulbs or no flash bulbs, I was going to send home some pictures of me out on duty.

Meeting my sister at Saigon Airport

This picture was taken of me standing in front a 2 man machine gun bunker in the sector I worked at Tan Son Nhut air base, unknowingly only a few weeks before the Tet Offensive. As the fates would have it, this was where I would be posted on January 30, 1968 and spend the next 2 and a half days, until relieved. President Richard Nixon would later sign The United States highest military unit award to the 377th Security Police Squadron, The Presidential Unit Citation on April 15, 1970, covering the period of January 31-February 2, 1968 for extraordinary heroism in connection with military operations against an opposing armed force. "Tan Son Nhut air base had suddenly come under attack from a large, multi-battalion hostile force using rockets, mortars, automatic weapons and small arms. The small 377th SPS, armed only with light weapons, reacted immediately, established strong defensive positions, and heroically held off the attackers during the early, critical hours until Republic of Vietnam and U. S. Army reinforcements could respond."

V. ADDITIONAL IDENTIFICATION DATA

1. LAST NAME—FIRST NAME—MIDDLE INITIAL	2. AFSN	3. GRADE	4. DATE OF GRADE
Markson, James J.	AF12765694	A1C	1 September 1967
5. ORGANIZATION, COMMAND AND LOCATION	6. RESERVE WARRANT OR COMMISSION AND AFSN	7. REASON FOR REPORT	
377th Security Police Squadron Tan Son Nhut Air Base, Vietnam (PACAF)	None	No Report for 1 Year	
	8. PERIOD OF SUPERVISION	9. PERIOD OF REPORT	
	100	FROM 27 Jan 1967	THRU 26 Jan 1968

VI. DUTIES

AFSC	DAFSC	CAFSC	NO. OF PERSONNEL SUPERVISED	UMD POSITION OCCUPIED	
				AUTHORIZED GRADE	AUTHORIZED AFSC
81150	81150	81150	0	A1C	81150

Current Duty: Security Policeman (Combat Security and Aerospace Security Forces). Performs physical security duties securing Priority A, B, and C Resources and other resources as required. Performs duty with Primary and Secondary Security Alert Teams. Provides preventive perimeter surveillance against Clandestine Threats and other duties as directed by the Sector Supervisor.

VII. COMMENTS OF REPORTING OFFICIAL (Be factual and specific. Add any comments which increase the objectivity of the rating.)

FACTS AND SPECIFIC ACHIEVEMENTS: During this period of supervision, Airman Markson has performed his duties in an outstanding manner; one which warrants praise from his supervisors as well as this reporting official. Airman Markson's job knowledge, ability to work under stress and without complaint makes him an outstanding airman indeed. During a recent ground, rocket, and mortar attack on Tan Son Nhut Air Base, Airman Markson's alertness, ability to stay calm, and devotion to duty helped the "newer" personnel from injuring themselves. Airman Markson's devotion to duty, conduct on and off duty, and dress sets an example that others would be proud to follow. He is an outstanding worker and readily accepts responsibilities that are handed out to him and seeks other activities that make him a better airman. STRENGTHS: Airman Markson's strengths are his personality, ability to perform his duties under stress with a minimum of supervision, and a positive attitude in anything he does. EDUCATIONAL AND TRAINING ACCOMPLISHMENTS: Airman Markson is a high school graduate and has one year of college. He passed his CDC and was awarded the 81150 in November 1967. OTHER COMMENTS: Airman Markson is of the highest caliber and it is recommended that he be retained in the United States Air Force, Security Police Career Field, and promoted to the NCO ranks well ahead of contemporaries. Airman Markson was nominated for the Air Force Commendation Medal for meritorious service between March 1967 and March 1968.

VIII. REPORTING OFFICIAL

NAME, GRADE AND ORGANIZATION	DUTY TITLE	SIGNATURE
PAUL F. WEST, SSgt, 377th Security Police Squadron	Squad Leader, Charlie Sector	DATE 27 January 1968

IX. REVIEW BY INDORSING OFFICIAL

Airman Markson is truly an outstanding Security Policeman. His devotion to duty, alertness, and calmness under periods of normalcy and emergency have contributed greatly to the accomplishment of this squadron's mission. I concur with the recommendation for his early promotion to Sergeant.

NAME, GRADE AND ORGANIZATION	DUTY TITLE	SIGNATURE
MELVIN G. GROVER, 1st Lt, 377th Security Police Squadron	Flight Commander, C Flight Security	DATE 28 January 1968

X. REVIEW BY OFFICER IN CHARGE: [X] I CONCUR WITH REPORTING OFFICIAL.   [X] I CONCUR WITH INDORSING OFFICIAL.

[ ] I DO NOT CONCUR. Airman Markson has clearly indicated through demonstrated duty performance that he is a professional in the Security Police Career Field. His ability to perform under enemy fire exceeds that of an average person with more experience. He should be promoted at the earliest possible time.

NAME, GRADE, AND ORGANIZATION	DUTY TITLE	SIGNATURE
CARL S. DENUZIO, Captain, USAF 377th Security Police Sqdn	Weapon Systems Security Operations Officer	DATE 15 March 1968

LAST NAME-FIRST NAME-MIDDLE INITIAL		AFSN	ACTIVE DUTY GRADE
MARKSON, JAMES J.		AF12765694	A1C

(CHECK APPROPRIATE BLOCK AND COMPLETE AS APPLICABLE)

[X] SUPPLEMENTAL SHEET TO RATING FORM WHICH COVERS THE FOLLOWING PERIOD OF REPORT		[ ] LETTER OF EVALUATION COVERING THE FOLLOWING PERIOD OF OBSERVATION	
FROM	THRU	FROM	THRU
27 January 1967	26 January 1968		

Precede comments by appropriate data, i.e. section continuation, indorsement continuation, additional indorsement, etc. Follow comments by the authentication to include: name, grade, AFSN, organization, duty title, date and signature.

ADDITIONAL INDORSEMENT:

The demonstrated reliability of Airman Markson while under enemy fire is noteworthy. I concur with the outstanding rating awarded in this report and recommend that Airman Markson be promoted in advance of his contemporaries.

[signature: Carl A. Bender]
CARL A. BENDER, Major, FV2226143, 377th Security Police Squadron
Squadron Operations Officer, 16 March 1968

AF FORM 77a PREVIOUS EDITION OF THIS FORM WILL BE USED UNTIL STOCK IS EXHAUSTED.   SUPPLEMENTAL SHEET TO AF FORMS 77, 707, 909, 910, 911 AND 475

Leaving Vietnam I would have a little over 2 years remaining on my enlistment. They sent me on my way with an "Outstanding" annual performance evaluation report. Major Bender was wounded by a mortar round, evacuated and returned to duty. This photo shows in order of appearance left to right, Major Carl Bender, LTC Billy Jack Carter, Captain Carl DeNisio, and 1LT Gerald Ingalsbe, courtesy of Tan Son Nhut Association. I would be honored, if one day they happen to read this book. I have the utmost respect for them and it was a privilege to have served with all of them. The bunker behind them in the picture is the 0-51 bunker where 4 members of the 377th SPS lost their lives during the TET Offensive. This photo was taken on March 20, 1968 during a memorial service for those fallen comrades. May they rest in peace.

Jim Markson VFW Post 107, Brooklyn,
New York Post Commander 2011-2013

CHAPTER VII

HE'S A REAL NOWHERE MAN
~ The Beatles

"Although both popular imagination and academic research on the Vietnam War continue to flourish, there is no consensus in sight. Only the U.S. Civil War rivals the power of the Vietnam War to divide and inflame generations upon generations of Americans."

~Andreas W. Daum, *America, the Vietnam War, and the World*

[7] September 1, 1967—North Vietnamese Prime Minister Pham Van Dong publicly stated that Hanoi will "continue to fight."

September 3, 1967—National elections were held in South Vietnam. With 80 percent of eligible voters participating, Nguyen Van Thieu was elected president along with Nguyen

---

[7] Vietnam source updates:
http://www.historyplace.com/unitedstates/vietnam/index-1965.html

Cao Ky as his vice president, the pair winning just 35 percent of the vote.

September 11–October 31—U.S. Marines were besieged by NVA at Con Thien, located two miles south of the Demilitarized Zone. A massive long-range artillery duel then erupted between NVA and U.S. guns during the siege as NVA fired 42,000 rounds at the Marines while the U.S. responded with 281,000 rounds and B-52 air strikes to lift the siege. NVA losses were estimated at over 2000.

October 1967—A public opinion poll indicated that 46 percent of Americans now believed U.S. military involvement in Vietnam to be a "mistake." However, most Americans also believed that the U.S. should "win or get out" of Vietnam. Also, in October, Life magazine renounced its earlier support of President Johnson's war policies.

October 5, 1967—Hanoi accused the U.S. of hitting a school in North Vietnam with anti-personnel bombs.

Tan Son Nhut
Vietnam

September 4, 1967

Hi Mom,

Here's some more green stuff to put in my bank account. Let me know what the grand total is now.

Hey, Mom, can you make any withdrawals from my account? I think I will need some for R&R. About that salami you mentioned in Sis's letters, go ahead and send it, but not a big one. Why not drop into Moylan's and see if Steve has any ideas about it? You might not believe this, but the house girl across the street makes the best hero sandwiches in Vietnam. The Vietnamese make bread almost just like the Italian bread.

About that bathing suit, I don't have an old pair of tan Levi's, so would you get me a pair and cut them about 4" down from the pocket? I don't want them to look like Bermuda shorts. Tell Sis not to bring a bathing suit. I haven't done any swimming in Saigon. I know there are a few nice pools here, but I haven't found them yet. What I really want it for is my R&R. Try to get a 29" waist for the bathing suit pants. I don't want it falling off. I hear they have a beautiful lake in Taipei, and I plan to do some vigorous water-skiing in November! Ha, ha. But you may have the last laugh. I've heard a nasty rumor that Taipei has a mild winter in from December to March. Try and send me a travel folder or at least some information about the weather there.

So long,
Diamond Jim

Tan Son Nhut
Vietnam

September 10, 1967

Hi,

I received the cookies about 4 days ago. They were delicious, only they came in about a thousand pieces. They got all broken up in the mail. But they were still good. How about sending me some more?

Thanks for that picture. The mail service was pretty fast. Yeah, I'm sorry I wasn't around to paint the house. But you know how it is when duty calls.

Hey listen, if you see Kevin around would you ask him to pick up 3 medium-sized Batman T-shirts for me? Or if you don't see him around, can old buddy Sis go over to the Bull Auto Supply store on Nostrand Avenue and pick me up 3 of them? It's on the opposite side of Kings Bay stores. I would really appreciate it. Along with those, I could use some heavy black socks or white sweat socks and about 3 sets of underwear, shorts, and shirts. About those cotton shirts, don't cut down the sleeves; just send me what you have.

Tell Sis that I have a friend of mine, a Filipino who works for Air America, and he wants to know if BOAC has a big maintenance place in the States and where it is. He's a maintenance supervisor and is trying to get a job in the States. Could she tell me where it is and if they would hire people from anywhere? Sis's days are numbered. Saigon will soon be upon her!

So long,
Jimmy

Tan Son Nhut
Vietnam

September 17, 1967

Hi,

Well I received two packages today, one with the peanut butter cookies and the other with my bathing suit in it.

There must have been some sort of mix-up about the bathing suit. I can't get it on. What size pants did you get? One thing though, you cut them right where I wanted them. Don't worry they won't go to waste. There's a guy from N.J. who should be able to fit into them. I finished off the sand cake the other day. Hold off on all this good food for a while and give me some time to devour it. No thanks on that Saucey Susan for chicken. I can't use it.

It takes about 4 or 5 days for me to get your letters. That sounds like a pretty good deal for Johnny Lund, but I wonder what they have in store for him.

I went over to Bien Hoa the other day to see Frasso and I ran into another friend of mine, Richie Spera. I don't know if you remember him or not, but he used to play in the band with Johnnie Costello, Billy Kisto, and those guys. He's in Frasso's company. He flies helicopters too. He'll be leaving in December. I also got a letter from Billy Golding, Kevin's cousin. He said that he's supposed to be stationed at Bien Hoa sometime this month? Pretty soon, everybody will be here.

Thanks for that booklet on Taipei, but it really doesn't tell you too much. Listen, ask Sis what time she is supposed to land in Saigon and that the only thing I'd like her to bring me is an inexpensive, small, and easy-to-carry puzzle ring.

So long,
Gentleman Jim

Reflections

My letter of September 17 is full of names of friends from Sheepshead Bay. All but two of them served in Vietnam, and those who didn't became New York City police officers.

I remember it well. I met up with Jackie in what had become our routine. He said to me, "C'mon, I want to show you something." He took me to a room; it was nighttime, and the room was very dimly lit and filled with smoke. There he was, Richie Spera, wearing sunglasses and playing cards with two black guys. It could have very well been a scene taken from "Platoon" when they were in base camp.

I had known Richie from the neighborhood. He was also not a wallflower, always up to and into all sorts of things. He played the bass guitar in a local band known as The Bards (the Beatles had everybody wanting to follow in their footsteps). On the evening of August 15, 1965, myself, Richie, and two other friends were among 55,000 people who would see the Beatles at Shea Stadium. The show made history, grossing an unheard of $304,000 dollars. It wouldn't be the only time we made history.

I can see him now on the stage of St. Mark's auditorium, belting out the opening of the Beatles hit "Mr. Moonlight". I even tried to weasel in on their act and became their manager, using the stage name James Holt.

Our lives had changed so fast and so drastically it was incomprehensible. "East is East and West is West and never the twain shall meet." It could not be said any better when it came to what we met in Vietnam. Nothing could prepare us for what we were about to endure. Likewise, nothing could prepare us for the reception we received when we returned. The very society that sent us now scorned and turned their backs on us. Even veterans organizations wanted nothing to do with us.

Hence the motto of the Vietnam Veterans of America, of which I am a member: "Never again will one generation of veterans abandon another." We mean it.

There would be no playing the guitar in Vietnam. Richie now played the M-60 machine gun as a door gunner on a slick, troop-carrying helicopter in the same outfit that Jackie Frasso flew as a door gunner on a gunship. Known as the Mustangs, you couldn't have planned this combination if you had a million years. They also shared another connection: They had both attended Brooklyn Tech, a high school that took a lot of brains to get into, specializing in engineering, math, and science. I don't recall ever talking about the politics of Vietnam, nor do I even know if Jackie or Richie enlisted or were drafted. It didn't matter. What we did know—and I'm speaking for myself—is that we had been dealt some cards in the game of life that were far from copacetic, that we knew for certain. We laughed when we saw each other halfway around the world, in a way saying, "Oh, no, they got you too." We knew that we were stuck here for a year and we'd do whatever we had to do to make it through. And we did.

Vietnam could be very intoxicating, as in the attraction a moth has to a flame. Jackie and Richie both took what is known as an extension. When their year was up, they would still have a few months left to do in the Army. Rather than leave Vietnam and have to put up with shined boots, haircuts, open barracks inspections, and more stateside pettiness, they both extended and—true to Murphy's Law—both of them would experience being shot down after they had extended. They walked away from it. Jackie, before he left, was awarded the Bronze Star. I don't know for sure, but if I had to wager on it, I would bet that the experiences during their stay in Vietnam left lifetime invisible and insidious wounds on their psyches that resulted in both of them taking their own lives many years later.

Richie liked to reinvent himself from time to time. In Vietnam, he wanted to be known as the Purple Baron, so we obliged and called him the Baron for short. I have no idea what the color purple or the baron had to with anything. Many years later, back home in Brooklyn, it became well known among friends that Richie had a serious drug problem. He grew his hair real long, had it straightened and dyed black, and wanted to be known as Tony Apache. He was playing in a rock band and wanted to look about 10 years younger than he was. He would seek me out from time to time and ask to borrow money, which I knew would never be paid back. Even though friends would scold me for doing so, I could never turn him down. I knew where Richie had been and whether it was for drugs or whatever, I could not say no. Although Richie was trained to be a helicopter crew chief, when he arrived in Vietnam they were short infantrymen and for the first few months, that's what he was doing. He more than paid his dues. Sometime in the late 1980s or early 1990s Richie lost his battle with drugs and, as far as I know, died from an overdose. He passed on, and his family quietly took care of business, with no wake or ceremony that anyone was aware of. Another casualty. And as sure as I am writing this book, an undiagnosed and untreated case of severe PTSD.

-Jim Markson

Where have all the soldiers gone, long time passing?
Gone to graveyards everyone
Oh, when will they ever learn?
Oh, when will they ever learn?

-Pete Seeger

Tan Son Nhut
Vietnam

September 24, 1967

Hi,

Well, as of 10 days ago, I became an old man in Vietnam.

I'm over the halfway point, with 6 down and 6 to go. Remember I told you that I thought I was putting on weight? Well, I was right. The other day, I finally got a chance to weigh myself and I tipped the scales at an even 180 pounds of solid steel. I'm a little flabby around the belly, but a few sit-ups will take care of that. See what happens when you're not a teenager anymore? You start to get fat. I just can't imagine me being fat. It worries me to death and, believe me, it's not from eating good food either. Talking about food, I think I told you I don't like peanut butter cookies. But thanks anyway.

Last week, they came down asking for volunteers to go to two different bases for 90 days. One of them was Vung-Tau. The other one was so small it didn't even have a name. It's a radar site near the Cambodian border. I would've liked to have gone to either one, but I have to take a test in October, so I couldn't go.

I received a letter from Johnny with some pictures of Drew and Kim. All I can say is that Drew looks a whole lot different from when I last saw him. In my opinion, he looks just like a little Johnny. What a fate to be born with! Please, one Johnny is enough.

I hope you can get the Batman T-shirts, as they will go over big here. One more thing, could you send me one more pair of black

Levi's pants, size 30–31? I could use them before Sis gets here. I only have one good pair of pants.

Tell Johnny that they don't have too much in movie projectors. They only carry cheap ones. But they do have movie cameras. I can still get that one that I already gave you the price for. I could buy it and give it to Sis to take back from her visit.

Talking about movies, when I was over at Bien Hoa, I saw movies Frasso took from his helicopter. He has real good shots of some combat missions showing rocket passes and the blowing up of sampans, bunkers, and all sorts of action pictures. They are really good. I wish you could see them.

So long,
Jimmy

Reflections

It was a nice feeling to know you were halfway through with the year you had to spend in Vietnam. I was not yet aware of that additional day I would have to do because of the leap year. Let's just say I was in a state of naivety. Not only was I not aware of the added day, I was also not the only one not expecting the fury of the TET Offensive that was coming in January 1968.

Once again, I was volunteering for transfers out of Tan Son Nhut, but it wasn't in the cards. I would finish my tour on March 14, 1968, exactly one leap year to the day, after I arrived.

Jackie Frasso did indeed have some amazing movie coverage of actual combat missions taken from the *Widow Maker*. After I returned home, Jackie came over to my parents' house and we watched them again. Unfortunately, they were lost in a move from one home to another, gone forever. Years later Jackie would continue taking movies in Vietnam when he returned for a visit. It was an extraordinary scene. Someone had arranged a sit-down dinner in a Saigon restaurant with former Vietcong guerillas, Jackie Frasso, and former U. S. soldiers as the guests. I wish I still had that video also.

-Jim Markson

Tan Son Nhut
Vietnam

September 26, 1967

Hello there,

I received the salami, socks, and underwear and Batman T-shirts. Thanks.

Listen, you don't have to send every package insured. They will get here. Don't worry so much.

Here are some answers to Sis's questions that she wrote me about in her last letter.

1. I'll meet her at the plane
2. I didn't make reservations yet. I'll make them the first of the month
3. If I'm not at the airport, ask somebody to show you where you can get a cab
4. You have to change all of your U.S. currency into either military payment certificates or piastres. But when you leave, piastres cannot be changed back into green, only back to MPC You'll change it at the airport
5. I don't know about travelers checks. They probably won't be accepted

Yes, I got the lighter, and I'm sure that I wrote and told you about it.

So long,
Jimmy

Tan Son Nhut
Vietnam

October 6, 1967

Hi Mom,

Right now, I'm getting things ready for Sis's stay in sunny Saigon.

I'll try and keep her pretty busy for those three days. I've got to check out this water-skiing place that I heard about a few days ago. This Filipino that I told you about has asked me to come with Sis to a Vietnamese wedding party. His landlord's son is getting married. I don't know if we'll go or not just yet anyway.

I got a letter from Aunt Margaret yesterday. It seems like all they do is move. They lived in Cherry Hill once before, didn't they? She said that she would be seeing you at a wedding on October 14. Here are a few more photos to add, in case you will be showing pictures to her.

These are just some pictures that Underwood took while he was trying out his new camera. The first one is yours truly and Underwood getting ready to go to work. Roger grew a moustache. I still can't grow one yet. The second one is me and a couple of the other guys. The one in civilian clothes is from Buffalo, New York. The guy in fatigues is from Newark, New Jersey. I don't know if you will believe me, but I didn't drink a drop. We were just posing to try out the new camera. The next one is of us doing the Asian squat. These people can sit like this for hours, and it doesn't bother them. Here is another one of me in the bunker during that attack on Bien Hoa. We were still trying out the camera. Some of them didn't come out too good because of the way they develop pictures over here.

By the way, I received your chocolate chip cookies and Batman T-shirts and the black Levi's pants. Thanks a lot. The cookies got here whole this time, and they were real good.

That's about it for now. Let me know how you like the pictures.

So long,
Jimmy

P.S. You don't have to use airmail stamps, as a 5-cent stamped envelope gets here just as fast. I found this out the other day.

CHAPTER VIII

PURPLE HAZE
~Jimmie Hendrix

"The Vietnam War required us to emphasize the national interest rather than abstract principles."

~Henry Kissinger, *Wall Street Journal*, March 11, 1985

[8]

October 21–23, 1967—March on the Pentagon drew 55,000 protesters. In London, protesters tried to storm the U.S. Embassy.

October 31, 1967—President Johnson reaffirmed his commitment to maintain U.S. involvement in South Vietnam.

November 3—December 1—The Battle of Dak To occurred in the mountainous terrain along the border with Cambodia and Laos as the U.S. 4th Infantry Division headed off a planned NVA attack

---

[8] Vietnam source updates:
http://www.historyplace.com/unitedstates/vietnam/index-1965.html

against the Special Forces camp located there. During the fighting, the 4th Battalion, 503rd Airborne Infantry earned a Presidential Unit Citation for bravery. Massive air strikes combined with American and South Vietnamese ground attacks resulted in an NVA withdrawal into Laos and Cambodia. NVA losses numbered 1644. U.S. troops suffered 289 killed. General Westmoreland declared, "Along with the gallantry and tenacity of our soldiers, our tremendously successful air logistic operation was the key to the victory."

November 11, 1967—President Johnson made another peace overture, but it was quickly rejected by Hanoi.

November 17, 1967—Following an optimistic briefing in the White House by General Westmoreland, Ambassador Bunker, and Robert Komer, President Johnson told the American public on TV, "We are inflicting greater losses than we're taking.... We are making progress."

In a *Time* magazine interview, General Westmoreland taunted the Viet Cong, saying, "I hope they try something because we are looking for a fight."

November 29, 1967—An emotional Robert McNamara announced his resignation as Defense Secretary during a press briefing, stating, "Mr. President...I cannot find words to express what lies in my heart today." Behind closed doors, he had begun regularly expressing doubts over Johnson's war strategy, angering the president. McNamara joined a growing list of Johnson's top aides who resigned over the war, including Bill Moyers, McGeorge Bundy, and George Ball.

November 30, 1967—Anti-war Democrat Eugene McCarthy announced his candidacy for president opposing Lyndon Johnson, stating, "we are involved in a very deep crisis of leadership, a crisis of direction and a crisis of national purpose... the entire history of this war in Vietnam, no matter what we call it, has been one of continued error and misjudgment."

Tan Son Nhut
Vietnam

October 16, 1967

Hi Mom,

Well, Sis's trip in Saigon is over now.

She has left here in one piece and much wiser. She has seen many things in only 3 days. I think it was a really well rounded trip. I got her on a helicopter ride to Bien Hoa. Although we waited almost all day for a ride, she said it was well worth it. I don't want to go into details. I will let her tell you all about it herself. I imagine this letter will get to you before she does. I will tell you one thing though: This is one vacation that she will never forget. She will be bringing a few souvenirs with her. Let me know how you like them. We had a little trouble with Johnnie's movie camera. I hope most of the movies come out all right.

How was the wedding? I hope you all had a good time. If I know you and Pop, I don't think you did, as you were probably worried sick over Sis being over here. Sis brought me those two puzzle rings. All I can say is they are really nice. When I come home, I want to take a ride up to the place and have him make me a really unique puzzle ring. A lot of the guys here want to order one too. I could go into the business myself, only I don't know how to make them.

Well, that's about it for now. Pretty soon, you will be getting an on-the-spot report from Sis, so I'll sign off for now.

So long,
Jimmy

P.S. Only 148 days left and counting…

Reflections

I was getting ready for my sister's trip. Looking back, it was very nice of the people in charge to give me the okay for my sister's visit, and they also gave me and another guy, who my sister remembered, 3-day passes to show her around. It's been my experience in life that even when people are in the same place at the same time, they remember things differently, especially after 47 years have passed. That being said, I sent my sister a copy of the October 16 letter and asked her for her thoughts, this is what she replied:

"I remember that trip as if it was yesterday. Rick and I went to an aircraft museum in Addison, Texas, recently and when I saw that same helicopter there, I knew immediately and remembered exactly where I was sitting before that guy told me to move to an inside seat 'cause it wasn't safe! What a bus ride back to Saigon! I remember standing on the hotel balcony at night after curfew and 'watching the war' in the distance. I sort of remember going to a local wedding celebration, but not too well. I remember that floating restaurant we went to with your friend Underwood from Texas. The VC blew it up a week or so after I came home 'cause it was popular with foreigners. I remember the taxi ride to that R&R place and playing badminton. Most of all, I remember watching you wing-walk as I left Tan Son Nhut and crying all the way to Singapore. When Dad met me at JFK, the first thing he said to me was, 'Sis, don't ever do that again.'"

Thinking about this, I wonder how many sisters visited their brothers during the war. Not too many, I believe. My father, true to character, was worried sick about having not one, but two of his kids in a war zone at the same time—and rightfully so. I cannot even touch the surface as to what he knew of war zones and trench warfare. The living conditions alone had to have been horrendous. I also find it interesting that my sister noted, "I remember that trip as if it was yesterday." There seems to be nothing like a war when it comes to getting your attention, and it never leaves you.

-Jim Markson

Tan Son Nhut
Vietnam

October 29, 1967

Hi Sis,

Well, I'm glad to hear that you made it home in one piece.

It was typical that you didn't have any money when you got home. Did you have a dime for a phone call? I thought Pop would really go for that "Boss" hat. Johnny must really be playing the role with the smoking jacket and swagger stick. I hope it doesn't go to his head. Poor Barbara. Hey, Sis, what kind of Seiko watch did you get? Thanks a lot for that lighter. I received the package before I got the letter. When I opened the box, I saw the film, ring sizer, and this pretty little box. When I picked it up, I knew exactly what it was. Nothing can be so small and so heavy, except a Dunhill lighter.

So Pop finally wised up and now wants me to pick out some wheels for you. I will check into it as soon as I can, but it seems that whenever I go over to the Chrysler dealer, he's pretty busy. I'll let you know all the facts, as soon as I get them.

Don't send me any more films. I can't find anyone with a projector that can fit your reels. I'll be sending them back in a few days. I'll keep my eyes opened for a good movie camera, but there's no rush.

Tell Mom that I sure could use that tan Dungaree bathing suit. This time, try a 30" waist. Also, can you send me some Bulldog wart remover? I've got one on my finger, and it's bugging me.

Here are some more pictures for that album.

So long,
Jimmy

Reflections

I was poking some fun at my sister. At the time, she kind of had a way of spending every penny she made—not a bad thing, just a little sibling rivalry. She didn't even have dime for a phone call? Yeah, those were the days.

I'm really glad she came to visit and realize now, although I didn't at the time, how unique it was. I remember the hat I got for my father, a military-style baseball hat with a lot of what we called "scrambled eggs" on the front with big bold gold letters that said BOSS on it.

I too had expensive tastes back then. The cigarette lighter I wanted and received was a gold butane, made by Dunhill. It wasn't cheap then, and at today's prices would cost you almost $700! Yep, that's right: $700 for a cigarette lighter. But I had one in Vietnam and held on to it for many years. Then one day, after I stopped smoking, I decided to give it away as a wedding gift to a friend of mine who smoked. I never mentioned to him the history behind the lighter as it was still during the period when Vietnam veterans were "hiding." He probably still has it, in working condition, without a clue to where it has been.

Before I even left for Vietnam the rumor mill back in the States had spread the word that you could buy a new car while overseas and get it cheap and tax free even. My father was interested, but it was one of those things that just didn't happen. It was far too complicated for me.

I remember that damn wart I had on the top right side of my middle finger on my right hand, the "saluting" hand, so to speak. I had developed this ugly wart that I eventually had to have removed at the dispensary. As a kid I had occasionally had problems with warts on my hands and would use Bulldog wart remover, but it didn't work this time.

Some of the things that I am reading now, 47 years later, I had forgotten about long ago, yet, with a little prodding, I remember them well.

-Jim Markson

Tan Son Nhut
Vietnam
November 3, 1967

Hello,

Here are more pictures.

These are of the barracks where I used to live. That is Underwood in two of the pictures. Rosales is in one of the others. As you can see, I'm making use of the Batman T-shirts. Here is also the recipe for that custard. I hope you like the way good old Peter wrote it up for you. Right now, I'm just getting set in my new barracks. Yeah, they're brand new. But over here, that's bad. There's no hot water or paved roads or sidewalks yet. The place isn't finished off yet. One thing good about the move is that, right across the street, they are putting the finishing touches on what you might call a shopping center. It will have a BX, supermarket, bank, bowling alley, movie, and mailroom all in one area. Yes, I did say a bowling alley. What next?

I received a letter from Johnny. He told me all about what to look for in a movie camera. I also got your letter with the $10 in it. Thanks, Pop. I still haven't found out about the car deal yet, but I will get to it, as soon as I can.

Did you see those pictures Sis took of Premier Key's presidential palace? Well, I heard a few days ago that the Vietcong tried to change the architecture while the vice president was there. I heard that the mortar tube blew up from a defective round. That is why the Vietcong only got four rounds off. If there were any articles in the news about it, would you send them to me?

So long,
Jimmy

Reflections

They built new barracks for the security police squadron. It was a nice gesture; however, there was one big drawback. It was military madness, more commonly known as a snafu at its best. Across the road from the new barracks was the Saigon heliport. All day long what flew in and out of the heliport? Yep, you guessed it, helicopters. What time did the majority of the security police squadron get relieved from duty? About 6 a.m. By now you know where I'm going with this. Yes, this was when the night shift, to which I was assigned, was supposed to get some rest and sleep. It was hot enough during the day, but now they added the constant noise of helicopters. Somehow, some way when you get tired enough you'll sleep. Well kind of. And I complained about no hot water. At the other two bases I was at, Phu Cat and Bien Hoa, there was never any hot water. On the other hand, the war was going well, so what the heck—why not throw in a movie theater and a what, oh yeah, a bowling alley?

Even as I'm reading my own letters I find this hard to believe, but nevertheless, it is true. I remember the movie theater well, especially after the initial days of TET. Things had changed, as there was a new sense of danger in the air, a feeling of constant danger. The movie theater was where we could go to escape and get lost in the fantasy world of Hollywood. The air conditioning inside, which was almost frigid, was an added change from the Southeast Asian heat and humidity.

Once again the rumor mill was working fine, yet I had to ask for news from home to find out what had happened only a few miles from the base. Vice President Hubert Humphrey was at The Palace during the mortar attack. No one was injured.

~Jim Markson

Tan Son Nhut
Vietnam

November 7, 1967

Hi there,

I received the letter and package from Sis today.

The pants are a good fit. Thanks for the other goodies too. The bathing suit will come in handy for my R&R and also for my skiing excursions up and down the Saigon River.

So Johnny said that I'm fat. I'm sure it was just a slip of the tongue. But lest we forget, I'll have to remind you that what may look like fat is really solid steel, and don't forget that, little brother. These pictures of me on water-skis can be used as evidence as to what physical shape I'm in. These pictures are the best ones yet, as far as I'm concerned.

I checked into that car deal. The dealer told me to tell Dad to get in touch with a stateside dealer to find out the details. I don't know too much about buying cars. He did tell me that you get an 18% discount. You put a deposit on it here and pay the rest when I come home and pick up the car. It would have to be bought in my name.

Tel Johnny that I'm sending Drew's Christmas present pretty soon in the mail. If you want to, he can open it to gift wrap it for Drew or wait until Christmas. It's up to him. Drew's is about the only present that I can buy here. The rest you can buy there. Let me know and I'll send you the money for it.

Well, I have to go see one of my friends. He leaves today.

So long,
Jimmy

Tan Son Nhut
Vietnam

November 18, 1967

Hey,

I don't know just where to start, so I'll tell you what I've received so far.

I got the Canadian coffee cake. It came after the poppy seed cake, but was still real fresh. You did a good job wrapping the stuff up. That poppy seed sure came as a surprise. I also received the pictures that Sis took on her trip. I want to know how the movies came out. I want a detailed report on where they were taken for the ones that do come out. I also received the Plymouth catalogue and I think that both the Fury III and the VIP are really nice. I think the VIP is a dressed-up Fury III, but I like it. As far as me finding out about buying a car here, I think you should forget it. I didn't like the dealer. He seemed to be trying to rush something on me. Long Motors seemed to give you a good deal on Sis's car. I think you would be better off sticking with him rather than maybe running into some red tape over here.

But about the car, if you do get the VIP, there are some things you left out on the Fury that I would like you to get, such as the fender-mounted turn signal indicators, rear-window defroster, and a remote control outside rear view mirror adjuster. As far as me picking out the color, I can't do it from a picture. I would like to see it in the flesh. So you take the honors and choose the color. There is one thing though, no matter what color you get on the outside, make sure you have an all black interior.

That's all for now.

So long,
Jimmy

P.S. Did you get the pictures of Big Jim on the skis?

Tan Son Nhut
Vietnam

November 30, 1967

Hello there,

I received your package of Christmas cookies and rum balls.

Rosales sure liked those Mexican wedding cakes. I think that it's a good idea about a moratorium for Christmas. But if I happen to spot something in the BX, I hope you won't mind if I violate the moratorium. I see you are still pushing to keep those apartments out. Good deal.

Next week, I go over and pick up my custom-made mohair and wool suit from Hong Kong. It's costing me $57. The suits are made by a guy named Lee in Hong Kong. They measure you over here and send him the measurements. They send the suit from Hong Kong. It takes a month for delivery. I'll be sending this one home, so you can get a look at it. It's a black one.

There are a few things that I'd like you to send me. First of all, a 1968 pocket calendar, and some flashbulbs too. And can you ask Johnny to pick up about four boxes of those Italian cigars called De Noboli, the ones that really stink and are short and stubby? One more thing, how about another try on salami? I told Sis that the last one was a number one and very good. Is there any more news on the car? Let me know.

I know that I haven't been writing too much. That is because I'm starting to get "short pains." That is an expression for when you are getting close to leaving here. I just don't feel like writing anymore…

I know that I'm not that short, but I'm starting to feel that way with less than 3½ months more to go.

So long,
Jimmy

Reflections

There was not much of anything going on, and that was evident in my letters. It was kind of a forced letter-writing effort to keep my parents feeling okay rather than not hearing from me at all. I sure was getting my share of care packages. I never forgot that and recently did my best to send the same to our new veterans serving in Iraq and Afghanistan. *I mention that a salami I received was a number 1. The Vietnamese had a numerical scale that they used to rate things. If you did something good for them you were a "Number One G.I." Something bad was a number 10. And if you really got them mad you were a number Twelve F-----G Thousand!!*

Just a little FYI.

I did indeed find an in-country R&R center run by the Army on the Saigon River. I had heard about it for some time, yet for some reason could never find it. I remember the first time I went there. I had gotten a taxi and the driver swore on a stack of bibles that he knew how to get to the place I had told him about. As we got further and further out of the city, the roads got narrower, bumpier, and muddier. There was even a moment when I thought that I was being kidnapped by the VC. I was alone and unarmed as per the rules—no weapons off base. Then all of a sudden the driver turned into a gate and there it was: GIs walking around in bathing suits, a Budweiser in either hand, a Filipino band singing "If you are going to San Francisco," outboard motor boats available for water-skiing! Sounds like something out of "Apocalypse Now," no doubt about it. Back home I was an avid water-skier. I lived for those summer months and water-skiing around Mau Mau Island in Gerritsen Beach, Brooklyn. Here, as in Brooklyn, the ski boat had to have a driver and a lookout to watch the skier. The only difference was that this lookout carried a 30-caliber, M1 carbine! Maybe it was for sharks—and just maybe these "sharks" wore black pajamas and carried AK-47s. Believe me, I am not making this up. I took my sister there during her visit, and she even remembers playing badminton! I wonder if the sight of the armed lookout deterred any of the prospective water-skiers. I doubt it. After all, this was pre-TET, and we were invincible. It's a strange place, that Vietnam.

Over the years, from time to time, the subject of the Vietnam War would come up. People would inevitably ask the question. What was it like? At first I didn't know how to answer, where to start. After much thought, I came up with the initial standard response of an answer. "It was the most exciting year of my life." To this day, I don't see any reason to change my answer.

And indeed I was getting "short"; with only 3.5 months, I was well on the downhill side of my tour.

-Jim Markson

CHAPTER IX

RED SKY IN THE MORNING

"Television brought the brutality of war into the comfort of the living room. Vietnam was lost in the living rooms of America—not on the battlefields of Vietnam."

~Marshall McLuhan, *Montreal Gazette*, May 16, 1975

[9]

December 4, 1967—Four days of anti-war protests began in New York. Among the 585 protesters arrested was renowned "baby doctor" Dr. Benjamin Spock.

December 6, 1967—The U.S. reported that Viet Cong murdered 252 civilians in the hamlet of Dak Son.

December 23, 1967—Upon arrival at Cam Ranh Bay in Vietnam, President Johnson declared "all the challenges have

---

[9] Vietnam source updates:
http://www.historyplace.com/unitedstates/vietnam/index-1965.html

been met. The enemy is not beaten, but he knows that he has met his master in the field." This was the president's second and final trip to Vietnam during his presidency.

By year's end, the U.S. troop levels reached 463,000, with 16,000 combat deaths to date. By this time, more than a million American soldiers have rotated through Vietnam, with the length of service for draftees being one year and most Americans serving in support units. An estimated 90,000 soldiers from North Vietnam infiltrated into the south via the Ho Chi Minh trail in 1967. Overall Viet Cong/NVA troop strength throughout South Vietnam was now estimated to be up to 300,000 men.

January 5, 1968—Operation Niagara I to map NVA positions around Khe Sanh began.

January 21, 1968—20,000 NVA troops under the command of Gen. Giap attacked the American air base at Khe Sanh. A 77-day siege began as 5000 U.S. Marines in the isolated outpost were encircled. The siege attracted enormous media attention back in the U.S., with many comparisons being made to the 1954 Battle of Dien Bien Phu, in which the French were surrounded and then defeated.

"I don't want any damn Dinbinfoo," an anxious President Johnson told Joint Chiefs Chairman Gen. Earle Wheeler. As Johnson personally sent off Marine reinforcements, he stated, "the eyes of the nation and the eyes of the entire world, the eyes of all of history itself, are on that little brave band of defenders who hold the pass at Khe Sanh." Johnson issued presidential orders to the Marines to hold the base and demanded a guarantee of success "signed in blood" from the Joint Chiefs of Staff.

Operation Niagara II then began a massive aerial supply effort to the besieged Marines, along with heavy B-52 bombardment of NVA troop positions. At the peak of the battle, NVA soldiers were hit every 90 minutes, around the clock, by groups of three B-52s dropping more than 110,000 tons of bombs during the siege, the heaviest bombardment of a small area in the history of warfare.

January 31, 1968—The turning point of the war occurred as 84,000 Viet Cong guerrillas aided by NVA troops launch the TET Offensive, attacking a hundred cities and towns throughout South Vietnam. The surprise offensive was closely observed by American TV news crews in Vietnam, which filmed the U.S. Embassy in Saigon being attacked by 17 Viet Cong commandos, along with bloody scenes from battle areas showing American soldiers under fire, dead, and wounded. The graphic color film footage was quickly relayed back to the States for broadcast on nightly news programs, giving Americans at home in their living rooms a front row seat to the Viet Cong/NVA assaults against their fathers, sons, and brothers ten thousand miles away. "The whole thing stinks, really," said a Marine under fire at Hue after more than 100 Marines were killed.

January 31–March 7—In the Battle for Saigon during the TET Offensive, 35 NVA and Viet Cong battalions were defeated by 50 battalions of American and Allied troops who had been positioned to protect the city on a hunch by Lt. Gen. Fred C. Weyand, a veteran of World War II in the Pacific. Nicknamed the "savior of Saigon," Weyand had sensed the coming attack, prepared his troops, and on February 1 launched a decisive counter-attack against the Viet Cong at Tan Son Nhut airport, thereby protecting the nearby MACV and South Vietnamese military headquarters from possible capture.

January 31–March 2—In the Battle for Hue during the TET Offensive, 12,000 NVA and Viet Cong troops stormed the lightly defended historical city, then began systematic executions of more than 3000 "enemies of the people," including South Vietnamese government officials, captured South Vietnamese officers, and Catholic priests. South Vietnamese troops and three U.S. Marine battalions counter-attacked and engaged in the heaviest fighting of the entire TET Offensive. They retook the old imperial city, house by house, street by street, aided by American air and artillery strikes. On February 24, U.S. Marines occupied the Imperial Palace in the heart of the citadel, and the battle soon ended with a North Vietnamese defeat. American losses included 142 Marines killed and 857 wounded as well as 74 U.S. Army killed and 507 wounded. South Vietnam suffered 384 killed and 1830 wounded. NVA killed were estimated at more than 5000.

February 1, 1968—In Saigon during the TET Offensive, a suspected Viet Cong guerrilla was shot in the head by South Vietnam's police chief Gen. Nguyen Ngoc Loan, in full view of an NBC news cameraman and an Associated Press still photographer. The haunting AP photo taken by Eddie Adams appeared on the front page of most American newspapers the next morning. Americans also observed the filmed execution on NBC.

Another controversy during TET, and one of the most controversial statements of the entire war, occurred when an American officer stated, "We had to destroy it, in order to save it," referring to a small city near Saigon leveled by American bombs. His statement was later used by many as a metaphor for the American experience in Vietnam.

February 2, 1968—President Johnson labeled the TET Offensive "a complete failure." For the North Vietnamese, the TET Offensive was both a military and political failure in Vietnam. The general uprising they had hoped to ignite among South Vietnamese peasants against the Saigon government never materialized. The Viet Cong also had come out of hiding to do most of the actual fighting; they suffered devastating losses and never regained their former strength. As a result, most of the fighting was taken over by North Vietnamese regulars fighting a conventional war. The TET Offensive's only success—and an unexpected one—was in eroding grassroots support among Americans and in Congress for continuing the war indefinitely.

Tan Son Nhut
Vietnam

December 6, 1967

Hi Mom,

Well, the other day I went into the orderly room to find out about where my next base will be.

It looks like I got hit with some good luck. I've got an assignment to Camp New Amsterdam, yes Amsterdam, Holland. It was my first choice. I put in for Holland and England. But of course, there had to be some red tape. About two weeks before I was called down, I was told that I would have to extend my enlistment 11 months if I wanted to go overseas to Europe, but they didn't say where. I told them politely what they could do with that. They then told me if I wouldn't extend, I would get a stateside base. But low and behold, my assignment came down anyway. I just hope there isn't a mix-up and they ask me to extend again because I won't do it, no matter where they would send me.

From what the lifers have told me, it's a choice assignment and that I'll probably re-enlist after spending some time there. Of course, there's no chance of that. I have to go to a briefing tomorrow about the assignment. I'll keep you posted.

I'm sending you the pricelist back. How about reminding Pop to put APO 96307 on the newspapers when he sends them? It would get here a lot faster. Another thing, it isn't true that airmail gets here faster. I received a 5-cent stamped letter from Johnny and it took a week to get here. Usually it takes about 4 days by airmail. I picked up my new suit yesterday. It fits perfect. I'll mail it home when I get the time. Have it cleaned for me, will you?

I'm glad to hear the movies came out. I can't wait to see them. Let me know if you show them to Underwood's girl.

So, Big John, the great white hunter went hunting? He wrote me about it. What kind of rifle did he use and where did he get it? I'd like to give it a try sometime. He told me he received Drew's X-mas present and it was a little too big. Well, better big than too small. Have you seen it yet?

Well, I'm going to give myself a Christmas present. I'll go to Taipei. I would hate to spend Christmas here sitting in a bunker pulling guard duty. So I decided that Christmas would be the best time to go.

I can't wait to find out for sure about New Amsterdam. Just think: On 3-day breaks, I can go anywhere, Copenhagen, Belgium, Germany—the works.

It sounds too good to be true. I'll find out soon enough.

So long,
Jimmy

Tan Son Nhut
Vietnam

December 14, 1967

Hi,

Well, I received all the care packages this last week.

I got the salami. I knew that it had to come from Moylan's. It was really good. I still have some left. The cigars were just what I wanted, and the flashbulbs too. I got a money order from Johnny as a combined Christmas and birthday present. Please don't send me any money here. Put it in my bankbook, will you? Thanks anyway, John. I also received that small tape recorder and tapes from Sis. It's real nice, but I hate to say that I'm too "short" on time to start playing around with tape recorders. I wish you had asked me first. There's nothing that I need over here because all I know is that I am getting short!

When did Dad decide on getting a Sport Fury? From the picture, it looks real nice and I'm sure it is. It ought to be real sharp in steel gray.

About inviting a couple of servicemen over for Christmas dinner, where would they come from? I think it's a good idea.

The other day, I found out I could really start working my points over here. There's a first lieutenant who is the duty officer for us who is looking for a handball partner. Of course, me being such a sharp trooper and an expert handball player, I was recommended. I haven't heard anything yet, but I'm sure I could get some fringe benefits out of it, especially if I let him win sometimes. But I'm too short to start playing dirty pool.

That's all for now.

So long,
Jimmy

P.S. How do you like the war pictures?

Reflections

Getting salami from Moylan's was a treat. They were a local butcher store that I had worked for before I joined the Air Force. Steve Moylan, the owner, had a son who had encouraged me to join the Air Force, as he did, and become an air traffic controller. It didn't quite work out that way; however, after my discharge I again spoke to Steve's son and eventually got the job after a 4-year detour. That's life. Don't get me wrong, at the time I was very angry about being assigned to the security police career field, but as it worked out I learned things as a SP, especially about myself, that I never would have known as a controller, and at this point in my life I don't regret it one bit.

This letter is dated December 14, and I was getting into the double digits: under 100 days left to go. It's obvious I was anxious. There is only one thing on my mind, and that is getting out of there and going home. That feeling would escalate to what I would like to call severe anxiety after the Tet Offensive and increased incrementally as I got closer and closer to my DEROS (Date of Rotation Stateside). No one wanted to get killed or maimed on their last day in country. It wore on me with each passing day.

If I remember correctly, my parents did invite a couple of servicemen home for Christmas dinner. I still think it's a nice idea.

I don't recall anything about the handball story with an officer. I do remember in high school I sure did enjoy the game and went on to racquetball later on.

Jim Markson

Tan Son Nhut
Vietnam

December 29, 1967

Hi,

I got back from Taipei yesterday afternoon and, to my surprise, I had some money left over.

I also had my paycheck waiting for me. This payday, we got the raise and it also included 3 months back pay, just the raise. So I decided to send a money order and save some of it. How about putting it in the bank for me? Thanks. Also, thanks for putting that $50 X-mas present in the bank for me too. Taipei was good for a change. It was nice to get away. The Chinese aren't like the Vietnamese. They're much more westernized and more modern, but they still try and get all the money they can out of Americans, especially if they know you're on R&R and have a lot of money to blow.

I told you when I called that I had Christmas dinner with an American family. I had a real nice time, better than I had expected. They were some real nice people. He had 3 small kids, from 8 years to 13 years old. He had a real nice house on Grass Mountain that overlooks Taipei. He works for the embassy in charge of Marines who pull guard duty for it. It seemed like I was in another world, being in an American house with American people and American food. It seemed funny. I kept thinking to myself that, "yeah, there really are places like this." It had been a long time. What surprised me was how easy it was to talk with them, as if I had known them for years.

I'm going to try to send my suit home today and also a birthday present for Sis that I picked up in Taipei. I hope she likes it. I'm also going to go over and get measured for another suit. This one will be sort of a green color.

When I called you, could you hear me clearly? I couldn't hear you too loud, but I could hear what you said. They told me at the R&R center to call from the telephone company to get a good connection. That's where I called from, but I don't think it was that good.

About the Christmas card I sent you. I don't really remember anything about it saying friends on it. Just what did it say about friends? I got a Christmas card from the Moylans with a $5 check in it. Good old Steve. I'll have to stop in and see him when I get back.

About my shipment to Holland, well there is a little cloak and dagger business going on. I'll tell you about it when I get home. Until then, I just have to sit tight.

So long,
Jimmy
That World Traveler
Big Jim Markson

Reflections

I finally made good on taking advantage of R&R. Even though Saigon at the time was like an R&R, it was a free trip out of the country and time off to do as you pleased. I had planned to go with other SPs, but whenever it came to actually putting in for it, they would back out, so I went alone. And once again, I had no regrets. This letter speaks for itself. After all it was the Christmas season and halfway around the world. And that Marine family who had me over for Christmas dinner, they were the best. I wish I could remember their names.

R&R centers were big business, no matter what country you went to, including Australia. The military knew this and made sure GIs who went to these centers were not unduly taken advantage of. Before I left for Taipei, I was given information on how to report any problems and, if serious enough, the establishment would be shut down. I had no complaints. I even felt a little guilty taking an R&R.

I also remember clearly the green sharkskin suit I had custom made, as it was quite a color. I remember the phone call I made from the calling center, and Steve Moylan from the butcher store sending me 5 bucks. It was great. And I was getting short. I had it made.

As for the cloak and dagger stuff, I remember it well. In the personnel section where all the paperwork was processed about our coming and going, there was an Air Force clerk who did the paperwork—an enlisted man like myself. As we were going over my orders, the clerk pointed out to me that if I wanted to go concurrent to Holland I would have to extend my enlistment for 11 months because it was a 3-year assignment. I protested vehemently. He then offered me an 18-month tour to Okinawa or Japan or Korea. I had enough of the Orient. I wanted to see Europe. All of a sudden, he took a quick look around and asked me, "What's it worth to you?" I couldn't believe my ears! I looked around too and made him an offer—I don't even recall how much. He accepted. Long story short, a few months later when I was processing in to Camp New Amsterdam, the clerk there noticed that I only have 25 months left on my enlistment. Too bad, chalk one up for me.

Jim Markson

Tan Son Nhut
Vietnam

January 11, 1968

I'm sitting here now, digesting that prune cake.

It was pretty good and real fresh. You sure wrapped it up enough. I'm glad Sis liked the bracelet, but I haven't heard anything about my suit. I sent it out the same day as the bracelet. Don't pay any attention to the prices I put down on the outside of the packages. You have to put certain prices on things so you don't pay tax or some other red tape.

Those two Navy guys looked like they just got out of basic with their short haircuts. From the letter, they seemed to have as good a time as I did at the Christmas dinner. The Marine sergeant that I was with said he was going to write you a letter telling you I was at his home. Did you hear anything from him? If so, I would like to know what he had to say.

About those Mikimoto pearls, I don't know if they sell them at the BX. I will let you know when I do.

Sorry to hear about all that cold weather. I'm off tomorrow. Think I will do a little water-skiing. That's life. War is hell.

So long,
Jimmy

Reflections

If I'm not mistaken, gluttony is one of the 7 sins. This letter kind of smells like gluttony to me—"sitting here digesting that prune cake," making fun of the winter weather back home, throwing it in their face with "I have the day off, I think I'll go water-skiing," and even joking "War is hell"—as if I knew! What I didn't know was that I was going to find out soon.

-Jim Markson

Tan Son Nhut
Vietnam

January 16, 1968

Hi there,

I'm glad to know you received my suit.

I would have been a little angry, to say the least, if it would have gotten lost. I don't believe in insurance. I thought I told you, but I guess I didn't. Yes, I received your $25 money order for my R&R and thanks. You can tell Pop to stop sending me the papers. It won't be too long until I'm reading them out on the porch again. The days seem to be clicking by at a nice steady pace with less than two more months to go. "Short!"

I hope the snow and ice lets up long enough for you to go and pick up Pop's new machine. I can't wait to see a picture of it. It seems that I picked a good year to be away. I missed the worst summer with rain every weekend and one of the coldest winters in a long time.

I got a letter from Johnny Lund. He is here. He said he is about 8 or 9 miles south of Da Nang. It took 12 days for his letter to get to me from Da Nang without ever going out of the country.

Hey, it's been a long time since I've had a brownie. How about sending a batch?

So long,
"Short" Jimmy

Tan Son Nhut
Vietnam

January 20, 1968

Hi,

I know that I haven't been writing much lately, but that is what happens when you get "short."

I think I told you in one of my other letters that I won't be writing much, so don't blame it on the poor old mailman.

I'm glad to hear it finally warmed up enough to pick up Dad's new set of wheels. I don't know why Johnny wants the Chrysler. With all the money he is making, I would have bought a Firebird or something along that line. I would stay with the Dodge rather than that Chrysler.

I checked in the BX about the Mikimoto pearls and they don't carry them. They have this other kind, Caribe. I don't know if you've ever heard of that line or not.

I got my income tax form for 1967. I made $201 subject to tax. The rest is all tax free. Could you send me one of those forms? I can't get one over here. Thanks.

A couple of my fillings fell out last week so I thought I better give the Air Force dentist a try. Well, I've never been to a service dentist before. He wanted to overhaul all my teeth after he did two of them. I had to call it quits. He gave me that feeling that he doesn't know what he is doing, and I don't feel like being a guinea pig for some young dentist right out of school. So I'll have to pay good old Dr. Duckstein a visit while I'm home.

I've got less than 8 weeks to do, so it won't be long.

So long,
Jimmy

Reflections

Obviously, there was only one thing on my mind: home! I just wanted to get out of there and go home. As I'm reading these letters, knowing what's coming, I want to yell and scream, "Hey, look out! You guys are about to catch hell!" But I can't. I just have to read on. There was some warning, but no one took it seriously. After all, this was Saigon, a secure area.

Jim Markson

Tan Son Nhut
Vietnam

January 30, 1968

Hi,

Well, I don't know if you knew about it or not but last night was the Vietnamese New Year called TET.

I've never seen or heard anything like it before in my life. All day long for about 2 days before the 30th, they were shooting off firecrackers. Last night from about 10 at night until 12 midnight, they really worked themselves into a frenzy. At midnight, gooks were shooting off their rifles. There were tracer rounds and flares and who knows what else flying all around the base.

I guess you know that we also had a truce here for the gook New Year. These truces are the most ridiculous thing over here. Before the truce was four hours old, the VC hit four Air Force bases with rockets and mortars. It makes a lot of sense to have a ceasefire, doesn't it? This holiday lasts for 2 or more days so we are going to be working different and longer shifts.

I received your brownies. That was a good batch. I also got the income tax form and sent it out already. I get back $7. Wow.

So long,
Jimmy

Reflections

Before security policemen go out to be posted, there is a formation that we know as guard mount. We line up about 4 rows deep, stand at attention, get inspected, and the non-commissioned officer in charge (NCOIC) will read off the postings and any important news that we should know before we man our posts. January 30, 1968, was the first day of what is known as Tet, the Lunar New Year. In Vietnam, it is the holiday of all holidays, officially celebrated for 3 days. There wasn't anything unnerving mentioned during the announcements, just a little about it being a holiday and there was going to be a truce and if I remember correctly we would be working a 12-hour instead of the usual 8-hour shift. No big deal. I had more important things to worry about, like counting off another day until I could go home.

And yes, indeed, there is nothing in this world that looks or sounds like the Vietnamese TET. I remember the first evening very well, I had a walking post on the flight line. I watched and listened in amazement at the amount of fireworks going through the nighttime sky. And yes, there very well could have been a mortar or a rocket flying in the air too and no one would have known the difference. I learned later on that the truce had been violated, but not in the Saigon area, and our 12-hour shift ended without incident. The next day of TET would turn out to be extremely different.

What follows comes from a variety of sources and memories that just may or may not be 100 percent accurate; however, after 47 years, it's the best and most honest accounting I can give of the way I recall things happening.

Air Base Defense in the Republic of Vietnam 1961–1973

The simultaneous, reinforced battalion-sized attacks upon Tan Son Nhut and Bien Hoa air bases were without precedent or sequel. So, in contrast to the hit-and-run tactics of earlier standoff attacks, the VC/NVA at this time aimed at overrunning and holding the two installations. The enemy meant to subdue the U.S./RVN defenders using sheer numbers.

To put you in the right frame of mind as to the magnitude and the rapidity of events that occurred on the morning of January 31, 1968, I will provide some statistics. Between 0320 (3:20 a.m.) and 1300 hours (1 p.m.), 23 Americans and 32 South Vietnamese lost their lives defending Tan Son Nhut Airport and another 86 Americans and 67 South Vietnamese were wounded. The total enemy body count (the counting action was terminated due to more pressing operational requirements) was more than 962. Tan Son Nhut was in big trouble, and like an old-fashioned cowboy movie, the cavalry and infantry saves the day, suffering heavy casualties in the process. Nineteen of the 23 American dead were from the cavalry and infantry units assigned to the rescue. To say I experienced a dramatic change in my perception of life in a war zone is a severe understatement. I made no more wise cracks about "war is hell." I enjoyed no more days off, sleep was hard to come by, my water-skiing on the Saigon River came to an abrupt halt, and the next time I made it to downtown Saigon was in January 2010, when I returned to Saigon—now known as Ho Chi Minh City—to experience Tet as it was meant to be.

Although the first night of TET was uneventful and we were working 12-hours shifts, things started to heat up ahead of schedule when, on January 30, 1968, at 1730 hours (5:30 p.m.), the base sirens went off. We assembled and were briefed that we were in Condition Red. Now I didn't know a whole lot of military terminology at the time, but I knew what that meant! Attack is imminent. It was another nice sunny day, no aircraft firing, no artillery, no incoming rockets or mortars—what were they talking about? I didn't believe it and assumed the lifers were just messing with us. Nonetheless, Condition Red it was. This created a posting problem of sorts for my NCOIC that would involve me. Fresh in from "the world" was a new airman first class (A1C), although I don't remember his name. Normally an A1C would be a security alert team (SAT) rider or given a post equal to the rank. However, this was like his very first night in Vietnam and no one knew what to do with him. So the fates decided to post him with me in a 2-man machine gun bunker as they couldn't morally put him out on a post alone. So the posting problem became my problem. We were inside a small sandbagged bunker with a roof of sorts. During the early moments of TET we start to see incoming tracer rounds from the initial attack, first from the east and then big time from the west as the VC tried to shoot down a departing cargo jet just lifting off the runway. Mortars and rockets were coming in, security control is barking out commands over the radio, and it was getting very scary, very fast. What did the new guy do? He panicked, chambered a round in his M-16, and pulled the trigger, firing off a round. I knew I was in trouble. Where did that round go? God only knows.

On another morning as fatigue was setting in from not sleeping, out of nowhere, two large dogs came walking across the taxiways, tongues hanging out, tails wagging, headed straight for our bunker. Things were quiet at the moment, and me being a dog lover I went out from my bunker to greet them. I don't know how to explain it, as it made no sense. I started to pet them as if there was nothing else in the world going on. The dogs were laid out flat, heads on their paws, when there was a *zzzzzzt* that went through the dirt at high speed. The dogs reared up, but I did nothing. Then two more *zzzzzzts* through the dirt. The dogs took off, and I realized that I was being shot at. I guess I was in denial—this was Saigon, damn it! You couldn't do that here! And I went back inside the safety of the bunker. I never could figure out where the shots or the dogs came from.

The captured North Vietnamese were pilots who, according to the plan, were going to fly American aircraft off the base after it had been overrun. There were unconfirmed reports that senior enemy officers had gone so far as to make dinner reservations in some of the finer restaurants in downtown Saigon! One thing was for sure. They meant business. One reinforced enemy battalion consisted of 450 to 500 men.

The O-51 bunker located on the very west end of the base was concrete and steel reinforced. It had originally been built by the French (we all know what happened to them) and was considered the most vulnerable point for enemy penetration, so it was manned by 5 security policemen and 5 South Vietnamese. Under the existing conditions it was thought of as a considerable defensive position. Enemy forces committed 4 reinforced battalions to assault this position. All 5 security policemen received the Silver Star for their actions that morning, 4 of them posthumously. The fifth was so badly wounded he was air evacuated to a burn center in Texas and received his Silver Star years later at a ceremony in San Antonio.

Ironically, only 4 days earlier I had the night off and was in the barracks when at 0025 hours (25 minutes after midnight) Exercise TET was initiated—a practice response to what was then a simulated attack on the O-51 bunker. I was a member of the responding quick reaction team (QRT). It was the one and only instance I spent any time on that doomed post.

There has been much written about the TET Offensive and the famous North Vietnamese General, Vo Nguyen Giap, who masterminded the plan. I never went to West Point, but I do know a little about numerical superiority, which was precisely the plan for the O-51 bunker and the rest of Tan Son Nhut. Yet the plan failed! Saigon Airport was defended by a lightly armed, mostly inexperienced security police squadron and was assaulted by 7 battalions of battle-hardened NVA and Viet Cong guerrillas. How could that be? The security police manning the O-51 bunker were able to hold off enemy forces despite overwhelming odds and reported desertions of the ARVNs (South Vietnamese soldiers) for a little over 20 minutes. Those precious minutes, which cost them their lives, allowed the rest of the squadron, armed and billeted in the barracks, time to roll the QRTs and establish defensive positions until reinforcements could arrive.

When you join the military, you are sworn in. It's known as the Oath of Enlistment:

I _____, do solemnly swear that I will support and defend the Constitution of the United States against all enemies, foreign and domestic; that I will bear true faith and allegiance to the same; and that I will obey the orders of the President of the United States and the officers appointed over me according to regulations and the Uniform Code of Military Justice. So help me God.

Maybe the planners of the TET Offensive were not familiar with this oath. To this day, I only remember one of our guard duty orders: "You will never leave your post unless properly relieved." And I'll say no more about that.

After spending a little more than 2 days on post and once things calmed down, a way to break up the squadron and get some relief going was established. The Vietnam that I had been accustomed to was gone forever.

The song "Time Has Come Today," sung by The Chambers Brothers, came to mind specifically related to these reflections. It is über Vietnam.

"Time has come today"
"The rules have changed today"
"Now the time has come"
"There's No place to run"

In Tan Son Nhut, the highest military unit award, the Presidential Unit Citation, was presented to my unit, the 377th Security Police Squadron. In a brief ceremony, Major General Robert J. Dixon, Seventh Air Force Vice Commander, attached the citation's distinctive blue streamer to the squadron guidon. The award, signed by President Richard M. Nixon, covered the period January 31–February 2, 1968, and credited the 377th SPS for "extraordinary heroism in connection with military operations against an opposing armed force." The citation read in part, "Tan Son Nhut AB suddenly came under attack from a large multi-battalion hostile force using rockets, mortars, automatic weapons and small arms. The small 377th SPS, armed only with light weapons, reacted immediately, established strong defensive positions, and heroically held off the attackers during the early, critical hours until Republic of Vietnam and U.S. Army reinforcements could respond." This marked the second award my squadron earned for meritorious service in the defense of Tan Son Nhut, with the first being awarded prior to my arrival. It took about two years to receive the citation.

-Jim Markson

Tan Son Nhut
Vietnam

February 1, 1968

Hello there,

I'm okay. Of course nothing happened to me. How about sending me a newspaper clipping of what they said in the papers back home? I don't have time to write right now.

Jimmy

P.S. Happy Vietnamese New Year

> ### Reflections
>
> On January 31, 1968, the Viet Cong attacked the U.S. Embassy with a 19-man suicide squad charging through. The Viet Cong temporarily occupied the grounds for 6 hours, until U.S. paratroopers and reinforcements landed on the roof of the building and the Viet Cong were all killed or captured. Pictured: Two U.S. military policemen aid a wounded fellow MP during fighting in the U.S. Embassy compound in Saigon, January 31, 1968.

CHAPTER X

STAYING ALIVE

"It is a key fact about American policy in Vietnam that the withdrawal of American troops was built into it from the start. None of the presidents who waged war in Vietnam contemplated an open-ended campaign; all promised the public that American troops would be able to leave in the not-too-remote future. The promise of withdrawal precluded a policy of occupation of the traditional colonial sort, in which a great power simply imposes its will on a small one indefinitely."

-Jonathan Schell, *The Real War*

[10]

February 8, 1968—21 U.S. Marines were killed by NVA at Khe Sanh.

---

[10] Vietnam source updates:
http://www.historyplace.com/unitedstates/vietnam/index-1965.html

February 27, 1968—Influential CBS TV news anchorman Walter Cronkite, who had just returned from Saigon, told Americans during his CBS Evening News broadcast that he is certain "the bloody experience of Vietnam is to end in a stalemate."

February 28, 1968—Joint Chiefs Chairman General Wheeler, at the behest of General Westmoreland, asked President Johnson for an additional 206,000 soldiers and the mobilization of reserve units in the U.S.

March 1, 1968—Clark Clifford, renowned Washington lawyer and an old friend of the president, was named the new U.S. Secretary of Defense. For the next few days, Clifford conducted an intensive study of the entire situation in Vietnam, discovered there is no concept or overall plan anywhere in Washington for achieving victory in Vietnam, then reported to President Johnson that the United States should not escalate the war, telling the president, "The time has come to decide where we go from here."

March 10, 1968—The *New York Times* broke the news of General Westmoreland's 206,000 troop request. The White House denied the story. Secretary of State Dean Rusk was then called before the Senate Foreign Relations Committee and grilled for 2 days on live TV about the troop request and the overall effectiveness of Johnson's war strategy.

March 11, 1968—Operation Quyet Thang began a 28-day offensive by 33 U.S. and South Vietnamese battalions in the Saigon region.

March 12, 1968—By a very slim margin of just 300 votes, President Johnson defeated anti-war Democrat Eugene McCarthy in the New Hampshire Democratic primary election, indicating that political support for Johnson was seriously eroding. Public opinion polls taken after the TET Offensive revealed Johnson's overall approval rating slipped to 36 percent, while approval of his Vietnam War policy slipped to 26 percent.

March 14, 1968—Senator Robert F. Kennedy offered President Johnson a confidential political proposition. Kennedy would agree to stay out of the presidential race if Johnson would renounce his earlier Vietnam strategy and appoint a committee, including Kennedy, to chart a new course in Vietnam. Johnson spurned the offer.

March 16, 1968—Robert F. Kennedy announced his candidacy for the presidency. Polls indicated Kennedy was more popular than the president. During his campaign, Kennedy addressed the issue of his participation in forming President John F. Kennedy's Vietnam policy by stating, "past error is no excuse for its own perpetuation."

Tan Son Nhut
Vietnam

February 6, 1968

Hi Mom,

I haven't been able to write you lately and that's because I've been working some pretty long hours here.

It looks like most of the trouble is over with, but Charlie is still out there and now the Army is hot on his tail. But they still don't know just how many VC are out there.

The whole thing started at Tan Son Nhut on Tuesday, January 30, when all of the Air Force bases in Vietnam were put on red alert. Red alert means that an attack is imminent. They had no intelligence reports at all that Tan Son Nhut was to be attacked, so everyone here was pretty calm. We went to work at 7 a.m. that Tuesday and I didn't get relieved until 10 a.m. on Thursday. Charlie started his attack here at about 3:25 a.m. on Wednesday morning. He started by firing at the fuel storage area at the northeast section of the base. This was a diversion as at the same time a 727 World Airlines cargo plane was taking off. As it touched off and started to clear the west perimeter of the base, the sky turned red with tracer rounds fired at the 727. This was the signal, and the stuff hit the fan all over the base. They sent missiles at the west side and mortared a gate there and started swarming in. They overran a machine gun bunker manned by 5 air police. They killed 4 out of the 5 men. The one they didn't kill, they beat him up pretty bad. After the second day, the air police had killed 109 Viet Cong on base. The Army and Air Force killed another 400 on the other side of the perimeter. A few Army guys got killed too. But that's a pretty good ratio in anybody's book.

As for me, I didn't kill any. I didn't even get the chance to fire my weapon. The only trouble I had was a few snipers. They were in my area for 3 days. But I could never spot them when they would shoot at me.

The paper inside is a pamphlet the South Vietnamese dropped by air over the VC. It's propaganda telling the VC how many have been killed and where and that they don't have a chance. I picked it up while we were making a sweep of where the VC had gotten on base. We didn't find any VC, but we did find a few mines that they had planted on base.

That's all for now. Send me some more clippings, will you? By the way, I received your salami today. Thanks.

So long,
Big Jim

P.S. There's a whole bunch of weird things I could tell you about, but I'd have to write a book, and I'm tired.

Reflections

Looking at the dates of the letters and the frequency I wrote home after TET, I'm a little amazed that I wrote as often as I did. The way I remember it, sleep was a very hard commodity to come by back during those days. It seemed like there was always something happening where the entire squadron would be called out and posted. My dates and times seem to be pretty accurate also. I can remember very well watching incoming machine gun fire that morning. I recall how whoever was firing wasn't afraid of being spotted; this was my first inclination that maybe this was not a hit-and-run tactic. Moments later my hunch became a reality as the cargo plane on takeoff roll lifted off at the west end of the airport. This was where the enemy had massed 4 battalions (2,000 men) to overrun the O-51 bunker. The sky lit up with tracer rounds aimed at the Boeing 727—how they didn't bring it down, God only knows. I would bet the crew needed a change of underwear when they finally landed at their destination. As for me, like I said before, I did not go to West Point, but I knew for every tracer round being shot up in the sky, there was an enemy soldier on the ground with a rifle in his hands, and they were coming on base!

As I'm reading this letter—and keep in mind it's written to my Mother—I'm puzzled by the "I didn't kill any. I didn't even get a chance to fire my weapon." We're talking about people here, killing human beings and I'm being apologetic. Like "Sorry Mom, maybe I'll get a chance to kill some people another day." What's wrong with this picture? Yet that was the mindset of the time. That's what you do in a war, isn't it? And during those chaotic moments that accompanied the assault, there were two episodes when I thought I was going to find out what it was like to kill a person or be killed trying to do so.

A sniper found his way on top of the roof of a two-story aircraft maintenance hangar not far from my bunker. It was during a lull, eerily quiet, when all of a sudden he let loose on full automatic and started spraying bullets at the aircraft parked on the flight line. He was to my nine o'clock position and less than 100 yards away. I considered it an easy shot. Without any thought, I left the bunker and set my M-16 sights for the roof, finger on the trigger, waiting for the illuminating flares to do their job. No sniper. He never fired another shot, and I never heard anything more about it.

One of the posts in my sector got on the radio, saying "They're headed for the F-4 parking area" (F-4s are Phantom Fighter Planes). The only thing between the post who made the call and the F-4 parking area was me, this time to the 5 o'clock position. I had a wide open field of fire, all taxiway! It seemed like it took an eternity for the flares as they oscillated, causing moments of artificial daylight followed by seemingly never-ending darkness. This time my finger was on the trigger of an M-60 machine gun. And each time the sky lit up, I expected to see swarms of Viet Cong headed my way. I waited and waited, with an intensity and focus that I never knew before or since. Again, there was no enemy. I never heard another thing about it.

And no "I didn't kill any." Now, 47 years later and maybe even a little wiser, I'm glad I didn't.

Although the base was declared secure Wednesday morning at around noon, it wasn't until Thursday that they figured out what was going on and could get people relieved. Indeed, there were snipers in and around the base. One of my biggest fears was when answering the calls of nature. I was dreadfully afraid that I would be shot when I had to leave the safety of the bunker to relieve myself. Nighttime was not any better because "spooky" was dropping flares all night long, continuously illuminating the base. All I asked was that if I was going to be taken out, please not with my pants down.

Part of being a Vietnam Veteran and the reception, humiliation, and disdain we received when we arrived stateside was another widely held belief associated with Vietnam: People thought that we were all drug- and alcohol-infused crazies. I'm sick of it. Were we saints, no, far from it. When I was not on duty, did I abuse alcohol? You better believe it. Were marijuana, heroin, and opium readily available within sight of the main gate at Tan Son Nhut? You can bet your life it was. Did some soldiers fall victim to what I call heavy drug use and bring it home with them. Unfortunately they did, but it was far from the norm.

But believe me when I say this: On the eve of the TET Offensive and during the onslaught that followed, the only substance in our veins was adrenaline, heavily laced with a sense of duty and honor. The overabundant drug and alcohol use is a stigma that has followed us to the present day, and I would venture a guess that I'm not the only one who feels this way.

I'm amused reading my last line: "I'd have to write a book." Some things take 47 years to get done.

Jim Markson

Tan Son Nhut
Vietnam

February 8, 1968

Hi,

How's everything going on the home front?

For now, that's enough about the war over here. Let's get down to some serious matters. First of all, where are those pictures of the new car? I can't wait to see it. Another thing, Happy Birthday, Pop. I don't want you to think that I forgot about it. It's just that the war got in the way.

I finally received a letter from those people in Taipei. It was a real nice letter, but no pictures. I was wondering if you had heard anything from them. It was bothering the heck out of me. I keep wondering why I never got a letter from them. They seemed like such nice people. I know they couldn't have been putting me on.

I got a letter from Johnny Lund a few days ago. He lucked out and got an office job. But even an office job isn't too nice when you're in the Marines. He said he's supposed to be moving up to Phu-Bai. It's on the map, but I don't know if he is there yet.

That's it for now. If you want any more war stories, you'll have to wait about 35 days. That is when I'll hold my press conference at the 2803 Batchelder Street mansion.

Until then, so long,
Jimmy

Reflections

From the first sentence, I get the feeling that I was just ignoring what had happened. How dare something interrupt my countdown? Didn't they know I was getting short? More than anything I wanted out! I wanted to get back into the routine I had going on, finish my 366 days, and go home. But that was not going to be the case.

I wish I that I would have saved the letter from the Marine sergeant and his family who invited me to Christmas in his home in Taipei, as it was a once-in-a-lifetime event.

Johnny Lund was a friend from Sheepshead Bay and was also in Vietnam with the Marines, God Bless them. Johnny's grandmother lived on the block that I grew up on. I came home on leave from Vietnam in March 1968, and Johnny was still there. I ran into his Father, Phillip, on the street. He was so glad to see me—and I mean overly glad. I could tell by the look in his eyes what he was thinking: "Please God, let my son Johnny come home in one piece also and soon."

Jim Markson

Tan Son Nhut
Vietnam

February 12, 1968

Hi there,

I've been receiving the news clippings from you.

I can see why you must be worried. But as usual, the papers have it all messed up and the facts twisted all around. I heard from Sis in a letter dated February 6 that you haven't heard from me since this started. Well this is the fifth or sixth letter I've written since January 31. There was some VC in the place where they store the mail to put it on the planes near the civilian air terminal. They had to use grenades to get them out, and it started a big fire. So maybe some of my letters were burned. I hope you have another copy of the *Time* magazine with the picture of General Giap on it. I want to save that copy. *Time* magazine is the only one that seems to print the nearest thing to the truth. It's the only magazine I read to find out what is really happening.

I hope you like these pictures. They were taken about a month ago. I got them out the other day. They were taken at a machine gun bunker and just by coincidence that's where I was posted during the attack. As you can see, I was pretty well protected and prepared, but nothing big ever did come off. I spent almost 3 full days living in this bunker, my home away from home. During the first 3 days, I got about 6 hours of sleep.

See you soon,
Big Jim

Tan Son Nhut
Vietnam

February 18, 1968

Hello, hello,

Well, I had a real nice Sunday today.

The VC hit us with 122 millimeter rockets, and I think a few mortars too. They landed all over the base. One hit the base church and destroyed it. I'm all right.

Don't pay any attention to what the papers say. After I read *Time* and *Newsweek* magazine, I have no faith in any of them now. I never read so much bullshit in all my life. Please excuse the expression, but it should be against the law to print that stuff. I'd like to go into detail about the two articles, one in the *Time* magazine that you sent me, and the other in the February 12 issue of *Newsweek*.

But I'm real tired after spending 14 hours out on post last night.

So long,
Big Jim

P.S. Did you get my letters from January 31, February 2, and a few more? I don't remember the dates.

Tan Son Nhut
Vietnam

February 20, 1968

Hi,

Well, they had another rocket attack here yesterday.

It landed a direct hit on the civilian terminal. Sis knows where that is.

Here is a money order. I haven't had much time to spend it, so I guess I might as well bank it.

So long,
Big Jim

P.S. Have you heard if Johnny Lund, Johnny Costello, and Billy Golding are okay?

Tan Son Nhut
Vietnam

February 27, 1968

Well, how is everything with you at home?

Things are still gloomy here. I received a package from Aunt Shirley and Uncle Frank about a week ago. They didn't put a return address on it, so why don't you thank them for me? It had some cheese, canned salami, and some canned rye bread. I don't know if it's any good. I haven't had a chance to eat it yet.

Tell Johnny he can stop sending me newspaper clippings. I'm tired of reading them.

That's all for now.

So long,
Jimmy

Tan Son Nhut
Vietnam

March 1, 1968

Hi,

Well, this will most likely be the last letter that I write to you from the good old Republic.

Here is another money order. I'm still working some pretty long hours and have not had time to spend it, so I might as well fatten up my bank book for Holland.

The car really looks nice. I can't wait to see it in person. I don't know about driving it though. The only driving I've done here is on a jeep, a ¾ ton truck, and a "mule." Don't ask me to explain what a mule is, but it's not an animal. Don't send me any more care packages because there is a new policy in mailing packages and they take a long time to get here.

You asked about that AIC on the address. They just changed the ranks around, not the grade. I'm still the same as A2C, but I'm called AIC.

Old faithful Charlie has been throwing his rockets in here almost every day, including this morning. It gets on your nerves, to say the least.

That's all for now.

I'd better see you soon.
Jimmy

Reflections

The letter dated February 12 speaks for itself. The letters dated February 18 and February 20 are the beginning of another new turn of events. Militarily, the TET Offensive was far from the sweeping victory the North Vietnamese and Viet Cong were hoping for. There was neither public support of the masses nor any uprising by the South Vietnamese population joining in with them. They were eventually defeated at every turn and suffered enormous casualties. But it came with a heavy price tag for the United States also. January 31, 1968, was the single deadliest day of the entire war. The military was willing to pay that price; however, hometown America was not, and eventually we would leave.

Although defeated in the TET Offensive, enemy forces scored an unexpected victory with the American media and quickly took advantage of it. The wake-up call came on February 18, 1968, at 0100 (1 a.m.). Enemy gunners launched a mortar and rocket attack on Saigon Airport, sending in 60 rounds, then again with two rounds at 1220 (20 minutes past noon) in broad daylight, again at 1520 (20 minutes after 3 p.m.), and once more at 1755 (5 minutes to 6 p.m.). The message was clear and aimed at the TV sets in the living rooms of America. They could hit Saigon, the heartbeat of the entire war effort, at will! They were far from defeated, and they played this card with great skill. From February 18 until March 14, 1968, the day I left, Tan Son Nhut would be rocketed 16 times! This was seriously upping the ante on my countdown to getting out of there—not only alive, but in one piece. And the closer I got to DEROS, the more the pressure would build. Time would slowly go by, and the rocket attacks continued. One night, while I was out on post, a rocket came in and exploded particularly close to me. There was no warning, just a blinding flash and the loudest *crack* I had ever seen or heard in my life. It had hit a fighter plane parked on the flight line, and everything around me was on fire.

I thought for a second that I was dead, thinking this was what it was like to be dead. But then the crackling and hissing noises of things burning brought me to my senses and I started feeling and checking myself. I had two arms, both legs, and I wasn't bleeding. When it dawned on me I was okay, I fainted and lost consciousness. The next thing I recall is the sound of the SAT jeep with 3 security police driving up on my post, letting the clutch in and out as it weaved through the debris. "Markson, you okay?" Oh, yeah Sarge…I'm fine. I was so "fine" that when the sun came up and things were relatively safe—or should I say, safer—I lit up a cigarette, took a deep puff, and put my hand down to my side. To my surprise, my hand holding the cigarette was shaking, rapidly. Only my hand, as if it didn't belong to my body, yet I did not feel it, I saw it! I sensed something was wrong, but never gave it another thought and it never happened again.

Another night I was guarding a command post and the outside buildings at the end of an alleyway. Outside the command post were several temporary trailers hooked up to diesel-powered generators. No one knew what was in the trailers at the time, nor did it matter. During the night, rockets once again came in. At sunrise, we left the command post and started to venture out to survey the damage. It hadn't rained during the night, yet we found ourselves walking through a clear reddish tinged fluid. The trailers were refrigerated, temporary morgues containing bodies that the main mortuary was unable to process due to the volume. One of them had been hit by a rocket. Yep, we were standing in embalming fluid.

I was even getting care packages from my Uncle Frank and Aunt Shirley. Uncle Frank was my mother's brother and the brother of Uncle Joe, the World War II veteran who had just recently passed away at the age of 94.

I would forever mistrust the media and the power it has to make a lie the truth and vice versa. You could spend your whole life trying to undo it, but to no avail.

My friends all made it home too—Costello with a Purple Heart award.

My last letter of March 1, 1968, kind of sums it all up: I was going to hunker down and do whatever it took to get through those last few days, no more care packages and no more stories, just let me out of there.

I remember my last night being posted. The tradition at guard mount was that the NCOIC—Tech. Sergeant Patterson, at that time—would announce who was getting relieved of duty that night and going home. It was a moment of recognition that we all eagerly hoped for. My moment had finally come and I was allowed to address the flight with some words of wisdom or thanks, and I did just that. Also part of the tradition was that you would be posted on some post and at exactly midnight, not a second after, a SAT would come out with your relief and bring you back to the armory, where you would turn in your rifle forever. It was a sobering event. Yes, this was really it! I was finally going through the last motions of getting out of the Nam. I was relieved of duty 3 days prior to my departure in order to have time to process out and complete the necessary paperwork. I had already done that, so I had 3 days to do nothing. I felt a little naked without my rifle, which had been a part of me, 24/7, ever since TET, and I was alone. I was the only one from my flight who was leaving. It was not a nice feeling at the time. Since the rocket attacks were happening so often and the barracks offered no protection, they opened up underground, concrete bunkers that had been built by the French for those of us who wanted to sleep there and be well protected. I tried it out for one night. I was uncomfortable with all the graffiti on the walls, written in French. Like I said, we all know what happened to them. Was the same going to happen to us? My last night I decided I would not spend it in the Old French bunkers. Instead, I spent it in my own barracks, alone with a bottle of Seagrams 7. Although my bunk was on the top floor, I woke up under a bunk on the first floor. In my alcohol-induced state I subconsciously crawled under a bunk for protection. I recall opening my eyes and seeing that the sun was up. I had made it through my last night! This was it! I was going to get on a Freedom Bird and go home!

The Freedom Bird that was taking me back to the world was a Braniff Boeing 727. The flight was full of GIs from all branches of the service who were also leaving. It was a stellar, bright sunny day. Needless to say, as we lifted off, as if rehearsed and on cue, a cacophony of cheers, tears, and profanities beyond description filled the entire passenger cabin. I was exhausted both physically and emotionally. I remember that, sometime during the flight, I put my seat back as far as it would go and kind of dozed off. A stewardess was in the process of putting a blanket over me as I slept. Still in my state of heightened awareness, I woke up, startled and fearful, and quickly pulled the blanket down, not realizing what she was doing or where I was. Then, in the blink of an eye, knowing I was safe and where I was, I went back to sleep. I wonder if she remembers that.

The flight was a milk run; we made several stops, picking up and letting others out all over the Pacific. It didn't matter; I had made my mind up I wasn't stopping until I got to New York. I remember going through customs at Travis Air Force base in California. The customs agents did not check anything. Rather, they waved us through with a big "Welcome home, guys!" It was a nice feeling. It was also a nice feeling to see my duffle bag with the same padlock I had put on it when I checked it in Saigon. The Vietnamese nationals were loading the bags onto the aircraft. I did not trust them one bit. I don't know for sure, but I think with all the time zones and delays I got into JFK International Airport early on a bright crisp Saturday morning. It was cold, but not too cold. I didn't care anyway.

I was purposely wearing my Air Force 1505's summer dress uniform and sporting my Vietnam tan. The airport was not busy at all, and I had no problem getting a taxi to take me home. I remember the cab driver, a grisly, tough, heavyset-looking older man, checking me out in his rear view mirror. "Where you coming from, man?" When I told him Vietnam, he replied, "You a lucky sumunabitch." Ah, New York City, ya gotta love it.

I had planned this moment many times. It was going to be a surprise. I still had the key to the front door of my parents' home. I got out of the taxi on the corner and walked to the house in the middle of the block. I quietly opened the front door and slowly walked in. I caught my father just as he was leaving the bedroom and heading to the bathroom with his back to me. When I called out to him, he turned and looked at me, then yelled out "Mother, Jimmy's home." Then in Dad's own inimitable way said to me, "Why didn't you tell us you were coming home? There's nothing to eat in the house." That would be the day! We always ate well, and that day was no different. The rest was unimaginable bliss. I made it home. It was no longer a hope or a dream. I was really home.

~Jim Markson

CHAPTER XI

BROTHERS IN ARMS

[11]
Vietnam War: Erosion of U.S. Military Power, 1959–1975

The roots of the Vietnam War lie in the U.S. Cold War policy of Communism containment, for it was containment that prompted the U.S. military to become involved during the First Indochina War (1946–1954) and to continue its involvement unabated until Saigon was conquered by the Communist People's Army of China in 1975. When actual U.S. military combat units first entered the conflict between North and South Vietnam in 1965, they were accompanied by huge logistical support by land, sea, and air. Such a powerful arsenal guaranteed that the U.S. never lost a major battle in Vietnam; however, the fact that the U.S. never achieved its objective of stabilizing an independent, noncommunist state highlights the war's significant complexity.

---

[11] Vietnam source updates:
http://www.historyplace.com/unitedstates/vietnam/index-1965.html

Although the U.S. military had superior military power, the communists waged an effective psychological "hide and seek" war in oppressive jungle conditions by using ambushes, night attacks, suicide bombers, snipers, and booby traps. Hoping to nourish the growing anti-war movement in the U.S., the communists also bombed key U.S administration sites, such as the Saigon Embassy. In addition, U.S. politicians' own political motives and their confusion about the war goals made it difficult for them to create an effective strategy in Vietnam. Facing pressure from strong anti-war protests, military policy shifted mid-war from battlefield victory to negotiated settlement and withdrawal. The soldiers perceived this shift as a further lack of support for the war, and reports of troop misconduct and demoralization increased domestic war-weariness. In a continued attempt to defuse the anti-war movement, the U.S. government ended the draft, but military technology could not compensate for the resulting decline in manpower.

Consequently, the U.S military was forced to reduce its spending on operations and maintenance and, after signing the Paris Peace Accord, ultimately withdraw from Vietnam in 1975. The war left the U.S. military demoralized and materially crippled. Defense spending dropped, and the power of the president to conduct war fell under attack. Because the U.S. failed to win its political objectives in Vietnam, the military's ability to use military force anywhere else in the war became seriously compromised. In addition, containment, at least as a military policy, was not a success.

Thus, although the Vietnam War did not end the Cold War, it did cast doubt on 25 years of U.S. military superiority.

In this chapter, a select group of our Vietnam Veterans have graciously agreed to share their stories.

Peter Griffin

My name is Peter Griffin, and I was born in 1946 in Oswego, New York.

I had six sisters (only one living now) and three brothers, all deceased. My father, William J. Griffin, Sr., was a fireman and civil servant clerk with the City of Oswego, New York. My mother, Leita E. Griffin, was a homemaker.

My maternal grandfather, William J. Lacey, was a U.S. Army veteran of the Philippine Insurrection and the Spanish American War. My brother, John T. Griffin, served in the U.S. Navy during World War II. He then joined the Army and became an infantryman/paratrooper and was killed in action in the Korean War. My brother, William J. Griffin, Jr., served with A Company, 1/188th Parachute Infantry Regiment, 11th Airborne Division U. S. Army at Fort Campbell, Kentucky. He and the other members of this unit were "atomic veterans" serving at Camp Desert Rock and Yucca Flats, Nevada, where they were exposed to 7 nuclear blasts in the first tests of close atomic support of ground troops. He died at age 57 after spending 25 years as inpatient at the VAMC in Canandaigua, New York, suffering from a host of physical and psychological disabilities.

I was a high school student before joining the U.S. Army, Airborne Infantry Unassigned, at age 17. I chose to follow in the footsteps of my two older paratrooper brothers and, hopefully, to fight the Communists in South Vietnam.

After the swearing-in ceremony, they flew us to Newark, New Jersey. I thought to myself, what on earth was I getting myself into? But before we touched down, I convinced myself I could and would become a paratrooper, no matter what! We were headed for training at Fort Dix. During the reception phase, we were literally shocked into the military lifestyle as they drilled into our heads that we were no longer civilians or "individuals" but government issues (GIs—i.e., government property)! One of the most traumatic indignities we had to endure was getting GI haircuts. Written tests would determine which vocations we would be best suited for, not that the results would be the deciding factor. The Reception Station was bad enough, but basic training was even worse. We rapidly learned much about discipline, harassment, humiliation, fatigue, stamina, endurance, and the need to follow orders precisely!

I trained in heavy weapons with the MOS of 112, 106 Recoilless Rifle (RR) specialist. I received orders assigning me to Company "I", 1st Training Regiment. Strict discipline was the order of the day. It was common practice for the whole platoon to receive punishment if even only one of its members screwed up.

When we successfully completed the AIT training program, we had definitely earned the right to wear the crossed rifles collar insignia and blue shoulder braid of the modern infantryman. I was now ready for parachute training. I attended Jump School at Fort Benning, Georgia, spending four hellish weeks completing the same training as my airborne predecessors. I then received orders assigning me to the 101st Airborne Division.

I served in Vietnam from July 1965 to June 1966 with the 1st Brigade (Separate) 101st Airborne. The two most highly contested actions I participated in were Operation Gibraltar and Operation Hawthorne. My military decorations include the Vietnam Service Medal with two bronze battle stars, the Silver Star Medal, the Army Commendation Medal, the Good Conduct Medal, the Republic of Vietnam Campaign Medal with Device (1960), the Republic of Vietnam Cross of Gallantry with Palm, the Presidential Unit Citation with Oak Leaf Cluster, the Valorous Unit Citation, the Meritorious Unit Citation, the Parachute Badge, the Army Republic of Vietnam Paratrooper Badge, the Combat Infantryman Badge, the Recondo Patch, the National Defense Service Medal, and the Expert Rifleman Badge.

During my tour in Vietnam (1965–66) we mainly kept in touch with those "back in the world" by writing letters. A chance to make a phone call was pretty much nonexistent! I never left Vietnam the whole year I was there. However, I did get a 3-day pass to Saigon once.

I received a warm, loving and private welcome home from my parents and the rest of my family. I became a full-time city police officer in Oswego, New York, when the war ended. I attended college part-time and after one evening class a few of us went to the Student Union bar on campus. They announced over the television that Saigon had fallen. All the students stood up, cheered, and drank a toast reveling in the success of their anti-war protests and efforts. I got up and walked out in disgust and revulsion! My time taking classes at that college ended as soon as possible after that. I did not feel I belonged there and never would.

My unit stayed in Vietnam. So, individually, I caught a plane from Phan Rang to Camp Alpha, near Saigon, for processing and departure to the States. We flew for several hours and then landed at Nakota Air Force Base in Japan for refueling and food. Our next stop was Camp Richardson, Alaska, again for refueling and food. Somewhere along our way, we crossed the International Date Line. We were going to arrive back in the

States the same day we left Vietnam. Our next stop was the Air Force Base at Charleston, South Carolina. When we got off the plane, everyone threw their hats in the air and then knelt down and kissed the ground. We were still wearing our jungle fatigues and boots. After showering, we threw away our filthy, stinking clothes and changed into our dress uniforms and left; we were on our own. There was no re-indoctrination of any kind. I believe our government knew quite well that many of us combat veterans from the Vietnam War would have problems readjusting to civilian life. There is no way they could have been unaware of the psychological difficulties veterans of previous wars exhibited after their return home. Most of us never received one minute of debriefing or counseling before going back to society. Perhaps if they did, many ruined lives might have been reconciled and many suicides prevented.

The military taught me to do the best job I could so I would never have to look back with regret; be just and fair with other people in all my endeavors and dealings with them; know the difference between true and false friends; and never forget those who have gone before me, especially those whose lives were cut short in the service to others.

I have wonderful memories of the beauty of the land and the courage of the Vietnamese people and ours. My experience offered the opportunity to realize how valuable life is and the chance to meet and come to know those who stood for what they believed in and were brave enough to lay it all on the line for the betterment of others. They were noble and unselfish souls, for sure, worthy of always remembering and appreciating the fact that you stood at their side and were blessed to know them.

The worst part was the deprivations of all kinds of comforts, constant exposure to the elements, and the need to eat cold, greasy, canned food, day in and day out. But the worst of all was the hunting and being hunted, not to mention the hidden mines and booby traps. My greatest fear was death, dismemberment, capture, and torture!

No, I do not regret going to war. It was a duty and honor to serve my country and to help one our nation's allies in their quest to be free. The only regrets I have are that our people were not willing to support us, and an allied nation and its people fell to the invading communist forces as a result. America lost prestige in the eyes of the world, and our enemies sensed weakness on our part. Chaos around the world was the ultimate result. We can thank yesterday's hippies for today's terrorists!

As far as protesters, if one does not support our troops or the war, he supports the enemy, period! I feel grateful when people thank me for my service and encouraged that they realize, at long last, that GIs do not start wars. We just fight them and we need public support so the government will let us win them! America should never again send its sons and daughters to war if it is unwilling to go itself!

Peter Griffin
101st Airborne
New York

> Many civilian non-veterans probably think that we glorify war, no on the contrary, we hate it. We just can't shake it and the horror that we relive every day.
>
> Peter Griffin is the author of *Thoughts, Memories and Tears* and *When You Hear the Bugle Call*. Visit his website Griffin's Lair at http://www.grifslair.com to view his many published poems as well. Peter recently received the Conspicuous Service Star with four accoutrements and the Conspicuous Service Cross from the State of New York for his patriotic service.

Morris Spitzer

My name is Morris Spitzer, and I'm a Vietnam veteran.

I was born in Yonkers, New York, on April 11, 1947. My father, Wilbur Spitzer, was a criminal attorney. My mother, Dorothy, was a homemaker. I have one sister, Nona, who is three years older than me.

Prior to being drafted for service in 1968, I attended the University of Maryland. I was the recipient of six All-American Honors from 1963 to 1965 for swimming and still hold the national record for the 60-yard freestyle.

I attended Fort Jackson, South Carolina, and Fort Sill, Oklahoma, for special training in artillery. I adapted easily to military life because my years of athletic training seemed to have prepared me for the organization and physical endurance required in the Army. I stayed in touch by writing to my family and friends back in the States. Once I arrived in Vietnam, I volunteered to become a radio transmission operator and forward observer in combat. I was in Vietnam from 1968 to 1970 with the Army 173rd Airborne, 1st/50th Mechanized Infantry Recon Scouts. At 20 years of age, I was the eldest in my group. I later joined the Short Range Ambush Patrol (SRAPS). There were no duties away from the front line, as I was in the jungle at all times.

During my tour, I lost 11 lieutenants. I received a Purple Heart for a shrapnel injury.

The witnessing of combat, casualties, and destruction resulted in anxiety attacks that came later. I have long been diagnosed with 100% Post-Traumatic Stress Disorder disability. I formed many friendships within my group. They were my brothers in arms.

The last 3 months of my 14-month tour, I was with the Delta 17th Cav. My family and friends were glad to have me back home in one piece. As far as readjustment to civilian life, I never felt like I fit in, but I learned to fake it well. My closest friends were not aware of my hidden demons, which surfaced many years later. However, I did self-medicate by smoking marijuana and experimenting with assorted drugs. But many of my friends participated, so I suppose that I blended in. Years later, I woke up in a military hospital in upstate New York, where I spent two years trying to recover. I then left to move to Florida and live with my mother, with the VA becoming my second home and safe haven. To this day, I still have terror nightmares, anxiety, anger, depression, and sleep disorders. I visit the VA weekly.

The wartime experiences were extremely traumatic for me. I grew old very, very fast. The worst part of the war for me was the constant killing and death. My greatest fear was getting wounded, dying, or seeing my friends suffer and die. The only good memories, if you want to call it that, are the friendships I made. I'm 66 years old today. Sometimes I regret having gone to Vietnam because of the suffering all these years later, but I'm glad that I served. I truthfully don't care if anyone thanks me for my service or not. I only have one thing to say to protesters: "Always have the soldier's back."

"It is not our abilities that show what we truly are. It is our choices."

I continue a relationship with one friend, Joe Salvati, pictured below in the photo with me on top. I'm not affiliated with any organization other than being a life member of the Purple Heart and Disabled American Veterans.

Morris Spitzer
Army 173rd Airborne 1st/50th
Mechanized Infantry Recon Scouts
Florida

Lawrence John Sheehan

My name is Lawrence John Sheehan, and I'm a Vietnam War Veteran.

I was born in Phoenix, Arizona, in May 1946. My father owned a roofing company, and my mom took care of the family. Dad was in World War II. I have three brothers and one sister. When I got out of high school, I joined the Marine Corps in June 1964 after President John F. Kennedy was assassinated. I chose the Marines because I felt they were the best. My specialized training was in M-60s. I found that I liked the structure of boot camp and became part of it—or rather it became a part of me. I was stationed in San Diego, Camp Pendleton, Okinawa, and Camp Hansen and served in Vietnam.

I engaged in countless patrols, firefights, and many small battles. On second thought, they were not small battles since out of 800 in my unit, only 47 of us returned to the U.S. I burned villages, killed people, and lost friends. I really learned to hate. Over the past 67 years of my life, it was the best and worst experience. Nothing can compare. I learned how to survive and endure. But the worst part was the friends that I lost and not being able to prevent any of it. After 'Nam, there were no friends. I left a part of myself there, and I brought a huge part of Vietnam with me. Every facet of my life has been affected. I was diagnosed with 100% PTSD in 2001.

My greatest fear was coming home. I returned from Japan back to Travis Air Base in the midst of the mobs of war protesters. As far as a reception when returning home, my family tried. But I could never feel it. The community's reception was filled with a lot of hatred and rejection. In 1967, I tried to join the VFW, but they said 'Nam wasn't a real war. It's sad to say, but I have never readjusted to civilian life—never have and am still working on that. Because of how I was received upon my return, my soul stills bears the scars of that reception.

After so many cold years and times, the country I offered to lay down my life for has begun to recognize the plight of its warriors. More than a few of us who served in and came home from 'Nam have survived, against the odds of rejection and negative labeling. In recent years, some of us have found help, some of us haven't. We still live with memories of darkness and death, ever struggling just to be, in the days that come and go.

In life and strengths forged in the fires of hell, we remain. And yet now we see mirrored reflections of ourselves coming home, a new generation of warriors, carrying within their hearts, minds, and souls the hidden nightmares of firefights, ambushes, and death. They are like me and have suffered, unspoken and waiting to become addicts with outward and inward hating, and all the many levels of abuse, of the self and others. Then there is that sometimes option of checking out altogether. We who have continued to have life know what may await the ones who are (and have been) coming home. Not all will fall prey to the downward path of PTSD, but many will, and more than a few already have.

I don't regret serving my country. But sometimes I wonder as my life has been so undone. As far as protesters go, I never had much to say except that I suppose they had to blame somebody. When people thank me for my service, my first response is to think they are too late, but I never say it.

I keep wondering if any kind of order will ever come out of the chaos of my life and the lives of my brothers and sisters in arms. So many upside-down backwards moments wishing that in our youth the country we pledged our lives to serve had not rejected us. For mom, the flag, and apple pie….

All that we thought was right became wrong, while through the doorways 'Nam opened, an endless seeping of darkness, finding all the cracks and crevices possible, for one and all.

Insidious in its delayed disruptive destructiveness, it remained invisible and unchecked, infecting and continuing to infect the nation I went to war for. We brought it with us, in the depths of our unknowing minds and hearts—indeed, undoing all we had been raised to believe in.

The un-doings go on and on. The American Dream is all but gone, as is the so-called nuclear family. Isn't this what the enemies of this nation have always wanted?

I am proud to be a former Marine and proud to be able to reach out, on occasion, to other vets, to the new warriors who are only starting to return home. We, of this country, have so much need to not just thank a vet, but to embrace them in every way possible. A handshake and a pat on the back are all well and good, but so much more is necessary for those who have offered to lay down their lives for this country. For the sake of truth, for the sake of life, let no more warriors be lost on their journey back home!

"Always walking on a thin line, straight off the front line"

In Truth and Sincerity,

Lawrence John Sheehan, Junior
USMC 1st Battalion Ninth Marines Alpha Company
One of the Legendary Walking Dead
Montana

> Lawrence John Sheehan came home in 1967, just as Jim Markson was entering Vietnam, but he was not diagnosed with PTSD until 2001, 34 years later, during which time he suffered depression and hatred that on occasion led to some interaction with the law. We applaud his honesty and willingness to share his compelling story. Lawrence would add after submitting his story the following: "A battle my life has seemingly been... a battle to live against a shadowy desire to exist not at all. I never really came home from the Nam. I never really let go of me at twenty. Disillusioned, fearful and full of rage, I never got beyond the rejections of my country. I became broken inside. I had failed and as such, I became a failure, a reject of life. I found ways to throw myself away by breaking the laws of the land and being incarcerated. I proved to society that they were right, and for me being punished was okay. I had become embarrassed of all that I ever thought I was. But I have awoken to the truth of me, and that I am more than all the wrongs I have done."
>
> Lawrence's sister, Susan Isabella Sheehan has organized the non-profit organization, A Circle Of Warriors to assist veterans today. She is working on gaining permission to have a satellite unit of her weekly meetings at the Montana State Prison, where Lawrence is currently incarcerated and can contribute in a positive manner regarding CPTSD, combat post traumatic stress disorder. Her website is: http://acircleofwarriors.org/

Dale Jordan

My name is Dale Jordan.

I was born in Chicago, Illinois, in 1950. My family consisted of my father, mother, and two brothers. Dad was a switchman on the Rock Island Railroad, and my mom was a waitress all of her life.

My father and grandfather were both in the U.S. Navy. Dad served in World War II and was a fireman on the *Old Saratoga* in the Pacific; he twice conducted A-bomb nuclear test dummies at Bikini Atoll in 1946 and 1947. His war stories had an impact on my young life. It was my reason for enlisting, although Dad was initially upset at my joining the Army instead of the Navy.

I quit high school in my junior year to enlist in the U.S. Army in 1967 at the age of 16. My friend and I flipped a coin at the recruiter's office and "heads" won out for the Army. I volunteered for Airborne training, went to war, got out at age 20, married, fathered children, and grew my hair long. Basic training took place in Ft. Campbell, Kentucky, with special training at jump school. I was uneasy at first, but adapted well later on. I loved putting on my uniform every day.

I was in Korea in 1968. In 1969, I was a SP/4 for 25 months with 2nd/506th/101st Airborne in Vietnam. We were in that unholy

A Shau Valley, Ap Bia Mountains, as it is known to the locals. If you have ever seen the movie "Hamburger Hill," you saw my Alma Mater unit in action pretty much on target. I wasn't ordered up that unholy hill, but was a radio operator in the valley below.

The worst part of my war experience? Enough said, as I like to keep my sins private. We did some pretty unspeakable things, which happen in war... I tried very hard to forget most of the bad stuff.

I literally grew up in the Army, from age 16 to 20, and was messed up in my head for many years afterwards. The life lessons that I learned from my military service were discipline and compassion. But I feared that I lost my soul there.

I was back at home working a new job at the Illinois Bell Telephone Company when the war ended. I had formed many close friendships in the military, but lost contact over the years. I did not belong to any veterans organization. I am so very proud to have been a member of 2/506/101st in 'Nam. I still have my glider/airborne patch on my garrison cap. We were the last generation to wear it, all berets now. I'm very proud of my cap. If I were born like 20 years earlier, I'm sure I would have fought in World War II. History was my favorite subject in school. And now I am very proud to have played a minor part in a major chapter in the history books.

I was proud of my country and put together a "war chest" of medals, badges such as silver Jump Wings, and CIB patches of units that I was in for my now 45-year-old son and grandson. I wish that my dad had done something like that for me.

When people thank me for my service, it feels great. I thank them for their thank you.

Dale Jordan
101st Airborne, 506th
Indiana

> Many civilian non-veterans probably think that we glorify war, no on the contrary, we hate it. We just can't shake it and the horror that we relive every day.
>
> The song "Sky Pilots" by the Animals (circa 1969) is about the chaplains who blessed our aircraft. I'm getting a little misty hearing this again and remembering the words "thou shalt not die" (my favorite).
>
> Sky Pilot
> He smiles at the young soldiers and tells them it's all right
> He knows of their fear in the forthcoming fight
> Soon there'll be blood and many will die
> Mothers and fathers back home they will cry
> ~Eric Burdon & The Animals

Denny Gillem

My name is Denny Gillem, and I was born in June 1941 in Sacramento, California.

My father, James Gillem, was an architect and my mother, Amy Gillem, was first a secretary and later a dispatcher for the California Highway Patrol during World War II. I'm the oldest, with 3 sisters.

I took Army Junior ROTC in high school, which likely influenced my choice of military service. After high school, I attended two years of junior college before getting an appointment to West Point. I entered the Point on July 5, 1960. I graduated with a BS in engineering on June 3, 1964, and attended Airborne and Ranger schools.

Although no other family members in my direct line served in the military, my grandfather's uncle commanded Gillem's Cavalry in the Union Army of Tennessee during the Civil War. There was another relative whose name is the same as my grandfather (maybe they were cousins) who was a general on General Patton's staff in World War II. Fort Gillem in Atlanta, Georgia, is named for him.

Plebe year at West Point was tough. I found that I really related to the discipline and value system at West Point—indeed, the values I hold today were established there. I am still close to many of my classmates, although we live all over the nation and some overseas. Life as a bachelor officer at Fort Carson, Colorado, was busy and fun. The BOQ was old but adequate.

After almost a year at Fort Carson, I was assigned to the 1st Infantry Division (1st Bn, 18th Inf) in Vietnam. I served as a rifle platoon leader for 6 months, and then I was selected to be the aide to one of our assistant division commanders. I then came home and was assigned to Fort Campbell, Kentucky, and the 101st Airborne Division. I was married en-route. I commanded Company C, 2nd Bn, 501st Inf. A year later, after going to the Detroit Riots, we deployed to Vietnam—in time for the Tet '68 Offensive. From there, more schooling and I was assigned to the Army ROTC unit at Stanford University, where I helped phase-out the unit. After more schooling, I was assigned as the Executive Officer of the 1st Bn, 26th Inf, 1st Inf Division (Fwd) in Goeppingen, Germany, for 3 years. We then went to MacDill Air Force Base in Tampa, Florida, where I was assigned to U.S. Readiness Command as a war planner for Europe and the Middle East. I was subsequently assigned as a professor of military science at the University of Tampa and then became an Army advisor to the Michigan Army National Guard. I retired from that position.

As a rifle platoon leader (1965–66), I was often in contact with the enemy. As an aide de campe (1966), I got to see the war from a new perspective. As a rifle company commander (1967–68) I along with my unit was regularly in contact with the enemy—very intense fighting. The last half of my second tour in Vietnam I worked in the division's operations center, keeping track of all combat actions in the division.

Although some of the combat events, specifically the deaths of some of my men were very hard on me—and I can re-live them now—I've had no problem putting that behind me and living a normal life.

I was engaged just before going to Vietnam for my first tour; I married when I returned. During both tours I wrote my fiancée (now wife) almost daily, and she wrote me and sent cookies packed in popcorn. I wrote my parents several times a month. There wasn't much recreation in Vietnam; I've always enjoyed reading.

Direct U.S. involvement in Vietnam ended in August 1973, while I was a student at the Armed Forces Staff College. Most soldiers served a single 1-year tour and then went home and got out of the military. Those of us who stayed longer usually had two 1-year tours (occasionally more). The end of the war meant nothing to most of us as we weren't involved over there at the time—and our nation just quit, there was no victory. A good question might be to ask us how we felt, having fought there, yet the other side won. This is the same question you can ask Iraq and Afghan veterans today. One of my fondest memories was the POWs coming home. My family was the sponsor for a POW family, and it was wonderful when he came home.

I flew home from both tours. The first time was for a few days with my family in California, then to my fiancée in Ohio. For my second tour, my wife met me in California and then had tonsil surgery.

There was much public dislike of our military at the time, but I never experienced any of it. I was with family and on military bases most of that time.

My combat experience made me a better Army officer and more committed than ever to work to keep our Army combat effective. I was and am very proud of our troops who served.

I returned from war with a greater understanding of my need for a relationship with God. The war experience taught me what real fear is and that I can handle it. I saw great nobility in the actions of my soldiers and others, including civilians. The worst part was seeing humans hurt and killed. My greatest fear was being very seriously injured.

I had and have great respect for those who will serve our nation. I truly respect those Americans who understand that with our rights as Americans comes a responsibility to serve our nation. We all have a duty as citizens. Honor is vital. No lying, cheating, or stealing. A love of country is important. These were life lessons learned from military service. I do not regret going to Vietnam, not at all.

Most of the protesters did not know what they were talking about, but that didn't keep them from talking.

My contact with fellow veterans over the years has been through membership in veterans organizations, but mostly through my West Point class. There has been some communication through the 101st Airborne Division association and occasionally with other groups. I'm a member of the American Legion, but not active. Most of my West Point classmates are in almost daily contact via email (server). Many of my company-mates from combat are in periodic contact and occasionally see each other.

After 22 years in the Army, I retired, found a job, and began my life as a civilian. I feel honored when people thank me for my service today.

Denny Gillem
Vietnam Veteran, 101st Airborne
Michigan

> Follow Denny Gillem on Frontlines of Freedom, a Military News & Talk Radio show that covers the most pressing issues facing our Armed Forces and veterans, in a balanced manner with challenging and conventional thinking.
> https://www.facebook.com/frontlinesoffreedom
> FrontlinesOfFreedom.com

Don Crizer

My name is Don Crizer, and I was born in 1946.

Dad was a World War II veteran who later became a mill worker for the Gary, Indiana, steel mills. Mom was a homemaker caring for my 2 brothers, 1 sister, and me. My father never said much at all about his war experience. Most of what I know about it came from others.

Prior to my entering the service, I was a journeyman electrician. I thought being a journeyman electrician would give me priority in construction or communications. I was drafted and entered service on April Fool's Day in 1969. Half of the inductees were drafted into the Marines. My infantry NCO training made me a candidate for infantry replacements on the front line due to multiple tours or death. My tour was under the 1st Air Cav, west of Tay Ninh on the Cambodian border. The cavalry was an elite fighting force on horseback dating back thousands of years. The term cavalry stayed, but instead of riding into battle by horseback, our group was flown in by helicopters that made it possible to drop us anywhere at any time. Our mission was to seek out substantial weapons/supplies caches being used by the North Vietnamese army. Our unit was on a continuous search-and-destroy mission, with one spanning 87 days straight. I was a squad leader responsible for some 19- and 20-year-old kids. My greatest fear was doing something that might get them hurt or killed.

While in training, the Vietnamization started—the political way of giving up. This rendered those of us there into agents stalling for time for withdrawal. Those that I killed and friends who died or were maimed suffered for no reason, contrary to the war of our fathers, who fought for a purpose. The worst part for me was realizing that the lives I took served no purpose. Going through their personal effects, letters, and pictures, I realized that they were no different than me. The following excerpt is from a poem written by Major Michael Davis O'Donnell while in Dak To, Vietnam. He was later listed as KIA on February 7, 1970:

"Be not ashamed to say you loved them, though you may or may not have always. Take what they have taught you with their dying and keep it with your own"

We were in thick triple canopy jungle on the Cambodian border when I got sick. Our medics hoped it was a flu virus because of difficulty of clearing an LZ. Then we needed an ammo resupply, which could not be kicked out as they hovered over us, like the food and water resupplies. In clearing the LZ, one of the trees that was blown over with c-4 fell on 4 troopers. A medivac had to be called in because of the broken arms and legs. They threw me on to be checked out because I was to the point where I couldn't carry my pack or walk. The fate of those guys getting hurt saved my life. I returned back to the States by medivac for convalescence. Severe peritonitis had set in after a ruptured appendix. At the same time, my NCO training roommate and close friend came home in a body bag. This was the initial setup for the survivor's guilt.

My discharge was in 1971. I was released from the Great Lakes Naval Hospital. I caught a train to Gary and called my mother to pick me up. After my discharge, I became a workaholic to forget. I mentally blocked everything for 40 years. While at the VA counseling for post-traumatic stress, I came across a trooper. He remembered both me and the medivac incident. His name is Bob Pullen. He contributed to the book *In Cambodia*, by Keith Nolan, which gives very accurate insights into what the Cav experience was. There is also a short documentary entitled "Shakey's Hill," by Norman Lloyd, in which our sister company stumbled onto the largest cache of rice and weapons in Cambodia.

The Vietnam War robbed me of a lot of family life. I am grateful to have an understanding wife who has put up with the years of post-traumatic stress. I hope to live long enough to make it up to her and my children. Living with the ongoing medical problems is a real pain.

Although I don't regret serving, I do regret going to Vietnam. It was a politician's farce. The politicians were reckless and uncaring with the youth of this country. But when people thank me for my service today, I am grateful and try to push back the survivor's guilt.

Don Crizer
Army 1st Air CAV
Indiana

In Memory of Don Crizer, a true patriot, who passed away in May 2014:

"The Next Place that I go won't be like any place I've been or dreamed of in the place I left behind. I will be free of the things that I held onto that were holding on to me. I take with me the love of those who loved me, the warmth of those who cared, the happiness & memories & magic that we shared. This light will shine forever in The Next Place that I go."

~Warren Hanson, *The Next Place*

Dedication

It is difficult to put into words the depth of my sorrow after losing my oldest and dearest friend from our Portage High School days, with him blocking the way for me as I got the football. The old saying was for 5 yards give the ball to Cowsert and get behind Crizer. I was with Don during the early years and the night before he left for Vietnam. We never had any time of disagreement, and we were always there for each other. The past 5 years we were blessed to travel with Don and Elaine and bind the friendship even tighter as 4 friends. Don was a true patriot in every sense of the word. He loved his country, his family, and his friends. With Don, you always needed your ducks in a row when discussing politics and views. He was not afraid to state the facts, and everyone knew what he stood for. I will especially miss Don because he was my brother by choice.

~John Cowsert

Delmer Presley

My name is Delmer Presley.

I was born in July 1949 in Pilgrims Knob, Virginia.

My father, William Hiter Presley, worked with the Virginia Department of Highways. My mother, Mary Lou (Tiney) Presley, was a housewife. I had 4 brothers and 5 sisters. Before entering the service, I was also employed with the Virginia Department of Transportation.

My brother Earnest was with the U.S. Army during the Korea conflict and my brother Elden was with the U.S. Army during the early 1960s, serving in Germany. I was drafted and went into service on November 6, 1968. I went to Advanced Infantry Training at Fort Ord, California. After the rough physical training, I was sent to Vietnam on April 9, 1969, and came back in April 1970. I was sent to serve my last 6 months at Fort Hood, Texas.

I saw a lot of soldiers wounded by either enemy fire or booby traps. I did not get too close to anyone over there, for they would either be short timers, going home, or get wounded, and I would never see them again. I also saw a lot of Vietnamese children burned (but still living) by napalm that the Army dropped from planes on some of the villages. The worst part for me was loading soldiers on the helicopters in body bags and seeing the Vietnamese people deformed by napalm. I will never be the same. My greatest fear was getting killed. I think the better part of me got left behind over there, somewhere in the jungles of Vietnam. I stay jumpy all the time, and loud noises really bother me. I have been diagnosed with Post-Traumatic Stress Disorder (PTSD). I had and still have a difficult time readjusting to civilian life.

My return home would take me through the airports seeing all of the protesters of the war at the air terminals. I wish that I could have asked those protesters why they treated us the way they did. We were only doing what we were told to do. I don't regret going. I regret the way it turned out. But I love my country and I would do anything for the U.S.A.

It took me a while to get to know my family again, even though I stayed in touch by writing letters home to my mom and dad. But I don't think the community as a whole ever accepted me back as a whole man. For those of us who made it back from the war, it didn't mean that our problems were over with. That's when a lot of the problems began.

When people thank me for my service, I sometimes wonder if they really mean it or if they still deep down inside condemn me.

Delmer Presley
U.S. Army
Virginia

> Delmer's daughter, Christal Presley, Ph.D., has published an incredible memoir about the unhealed wounds of war and their impact on the children of veterans in her book *Thirty Days with My Father: Finding Peace From Wartime PTSD*.

John J. Coppinger

My name is John J. Coppinger. I was born August 1945 in Brooklyn, New York.

My mother was a housewife, and my father was a New York City fireman with two other jobs. I have 4 brothers and 4 sisters. My brother Thomas did two tours in Vietnam with the U.S. Special Forces, and Richard did one tour in Vietnam as a U.S. Marine.

I wanted to go Airborne and enlisted after high school with Special Forces. The early days of training were spent at Fort Dix for basic and AIT training, then on to Fort Benning for jump school. I received specialized training in light and heavy weapons and operation and intelligence. I served in Vietnam from January 1966 to May 1968. Our unit was a Mobile Guerilla Unit and was called upon for different operations. I am in the photo with the Cambodian mercenary troops. I had just stolen that jeep, and we had finished putting our markings on it. I was securing an area where we hooked up an 8" shell to a radio; if the VC found it and touched the dial, it would blow. Note the scarves in the photo. The red, white, and blue scarves were given to us so when extracted from a HOT LZ, the chopper pilots would not mistake us for NVA or VC. The Cambodians were paid about $30 a month. If they got a good kill or turned in an enemy weapon, they would get a bonus. This was Tay Nint Operations Base. We had a camp outside at Trung Sup near Nuiba Den Mountain.

The worst part of my time in Vietnam was being depressed about having people you know and friends be wounded or killed in action. The men that I served with will always be in my prayers. I consider them my brothers. But I did form friendships in my unit. We still keep in touch 47 years later, attend reunions, and tell the biggest "lies." I have been a member of the Special Forces Association for more than 20 years and Special Operations Association for more than 10 years. We go to reunions every 2 or 3 years, all over the United States.

I stayed in touch with my family through letters and, when I returned home, the reception was great. But I was upset that I was going back to take a civilian contractor job in Vietnam. I met and married a Vietnamese woman and lived in Vietnam for 10 years. This ultimately led to a divorce and my returning back to the States.

When the Vietnam War ended in 1975, I was back in the U.S. living in Orlando, Florida. I was changed by my war experience by realizing that life passes by in the blink of an eye and we need to live it to the fullest and honor Jesus. I do not regret going though and am very proud to have served. My only feeling about the protesters of that war is that they have to live with their decisions.

John J. Coppinger
U.S. Army Special Operations
Florida

John Sutor

My name is John Sutor, and I am a Vietnam veteran.

I was born in Trenton, New Jersey, in 1946. My mom worked as a riveter during World War II. My dad was in the Second Infantry Division Rock of the Marne and landed on Omaha Beach on June 6, 1944. He was captured sometime after the invasion, escaped, and was then recaptured several weeks later, spending the remainder of the war in different concentration camps. I met with POWs who were prisoners with him at a POW reunion. Dad developed a mean streak and became an alcoholic. He was a union carpenter after the war, but he did manage to go to work every day.

I had a brother who was 9 years younger who died at age 27 from a drug overdose. My sister and I are estranged. She is married to an anti-war activist that I came very close to hurting badly after an argument in 1969.

In 1962, I quit school in the ninth grade after repeating eighth grade and then repeating ninth. I worked with my dad as a laborer. We worked all over the East Coast. We spent many weeks away from home and would come home sometimes one weekend a month. He worked for Henkle and McCoys for 30 years. He and I just didn't get along, so one day in September 1964 I quit and joined the Army. My enlistment date was October 14, 1964.

Choosing the Army was mostly generated through my family members' service. My friend's dad was in the 11th Airborne during World War II. He influenced me to join the paratroopers. My Uncle Frank served in the Army in North Africa during World War II. My Uncle Ed was in the Merchant Marines and made several trips through the Murmansk run. He married my mom's sister.

My specialized training was in Airborne infantry. Adapting to military life didn't come easy, as I was a smart ass, just as I had been in school. I made it through basic training in Ft. Dix, New Jersey. My mom and a lady friend showed up during PT one day, and I was completely humiliated. How they got on base I never found out. After they left, my company commander called me in front of the entire company and said, "You see this boy? His momma came here for a visit, but little does he know that he lost his momma and his daddy the day he joined this Army. We are all the family you will need!"

Then I went to Ft. Jackson, South Carolina, for AIT, received an article 15 for fighting, was brought up to Plt. Leader Sergeant First Class Hill, and was told that I may not be able to go to jump school if I didn't straighten out. He was a Ranger Path Finder. Punishment was 14 days of cleaning grease pits at the mess hall starting at 0400 hours. I made it through AIT, and the article 15 did not follow me to jump school. Jump school was right up my alley. I loved PT and running. Guys would be dropping out left and right, but I was determined to make it through. I guess

I needed to prove to myself that I had the right stuff. I made my fifth jump for my wings on my birthday, March 6, 1965.

Then I was assigned to the 101st Ft. Campbell, Kentucky, in B Company, 1st 502nd. I was very proud to become a paratrooper. I met Larry Ganns, who took me under his wing. He was a short timer and was getting out after spending almost 9 years in the service. That's when I learned about Vietnam and Cambodia. He had done a tour in Southeast Asia and told me that the "shit is about to hit the fan" and that he would not be re-enlisting.

Larry Ganns would explain what he had witnessed several months prior to our arrival. He had spent weeks in the jungles of Cambodia and Vietnam as a recon observer and photo-journalist. There was nothing secret. He was attached to headquarters as an observer and to photo document terrain and possible rear areas for possible rear area headquarters. This was in early March 1965. In the following weeks in early June 1965, we spent many hours at the range firing various weapons. We completed both day and night jumps with full gear and PAE bags. The rumors were rampant, but would come to fruition in the next few weeks.

We were called to a general assembly with Company Commander Antonio Mavroudis, who gave us the speech that many commanders must have given their troops before leaving for war. We were not shocked by the message, but more shocked by the time limit we had to get our gear ready and move out. We were told to give our loved ones a call and to say we would be leaving for Vietnam within the week.

I can remember only a few words from his speech. The ones that stick out in my mind the most are: "If I tell you to go out there and die, you will go and die. You will be remembered for your honor and duty to your country. Dismissed." After several tours, Major Antonio Michael Mavoudis was killed in action on October 28, 1967.

After we were dismissed, our leader came into our barracks and called 5 guys from our unit, including me and Jim Finnerty. We were friends from jump school. We were lined up and as he passed by shaking his head with a half-smile on his face he said to us, "You 5 are the luckiest bastards in this company. You aren't going to 'Nam yet. You were picked to go on 90 days (SD) to West Point to train cadets." We all were excited, but also felt a certain amount of guilt. But as soon as our SD was completed, we would be joining them in Vietnam. We returned in late September to a very bare barracks, just a few short timers who were not going to 'Nam. They told us that there was no way they were going to re-enlist.

We hung around until the end of October and then received our orders for 'Nam. I was to go to A Company/2nd/ 502nd, and Jim was to go to B Company 1st of the 327th. We were granted a 30-day leave prior to departure to 'Nam. Jim went home to Edison, New Jersey, and I to the home that I am sitting in now as I write this story more than 40 years later. I'm thinking I sure didn't get too far in the last 48 years. Anyway, I spent the next 30 days hanging with my school friends who had managed to graduate but were worried about the draft. Some of the guys enlisted, and some waited for the lottery to get them.

There was much on the news every night about the fighting and Mom was worried. Dad was dad. He never showed any true emotion about me leaving for war. I really never found out how he felt until I received a letter from him sometime later. It was my twentieth birthday, and we were deep in the shit on the Cambodian border.

The 30-day leave went remarkably fast. Dad bought my ticket and Jim's ticket with the understanding that he would repay my father, which he did at Oakland airport. The night before leaving, the friends that I grew up with had a going away party. We went to a friend's farmhouse that is still there today, and every time I drive by I get a flashback of that night that we drank ourselves into oblivion. I can't really say how I made it home. But I can remember drinking straight vodka.

Dad and Mom, brother and sister were home. But I can't remember whether anyone showed much if any emotion over our leaving for war. Maybe they just didn't understand the scope of the war. The news covered the troop build-up and the battles that our unit was engaged in. Jim had somehow received information that several of the guys in our company had been killed in a battle at the Michalin rubber plantation. I'm thinking that they (the KIAs) were from a town close to him. Dad and Mr. Finnerty were busy talking about their time spent in the service, and Mom had put out a lunch.

I loaded my duffle bag into the trunk of Mr. Finnerty's car, and we headed out. A couple of hugs with no crying or last words of wisdom from Dad and off we went. Mr. Finnerty tried to keep a conversation going while on the trip to the airport, mostly about when we get home and the weather. After dropping us off, he shook our hands and drove off as though we were leaving for vacation. I don't really know what type of emotion should have taken place, and back then it could have been the norm.

Our first stop was the Dallas airport and then off to Oakland. As we were approaching Oakland, the plane was having trouble with the landing gear and the stewards asked that we assume the crash positions. But first they would need to collect all shoes from the passengers. That must have been protocol back in 1965. They asked Jim and I to help collect the shoes and place them in the back of the plane. The landing gear was down, but the control panel was showing that it was not locked. They came over the speaker to assume the crash position as we had been shown, bending over and putting our heads down as low as we could, with our hands behind our necks. I can remember Jim saying that were going to die before we even got to 'Nam. I am laughing now as I'm writing, but it wasn't funny then. Well, as it turned out the gear was locked, and we landed unscathed.

There was a bus waiting for us and many other troops to be processed, with a wait time of up to 3 weeks before leaving for the country. That brought us close to Christmas time. We were permitted off base and went into San Francisco a couple times. I remember going to two bars: Big Al's and the other was the Red Balloon.

In the first months of deployment, it was rough to say the least. One day you are sitting there with a squad member, and the next you were loading his body onto a chopper with his face blown off. You become hardened, and even to this day I feel the same way about death. When Dad died, it was like, "okay he's gone." It was like he went to Florida and I haven't heard from him since December 1993. Yet when we had to put one of our pooches down, I cried like a baby.

I know it comes from so much death and destruction. Killing became easy. They were no more than targets. I was sure that we were no more than targets to them too. That was my thinking at the time. I had no respect for the enemies because I just wanted to kill as many as I could and get out alive. I would take trophies from their bodies and pass them out. Yes, that person is still in me, but has been under control for the last 48 years. I think the only thing that would flip the switch on is anyone hurting my grandchildren or my wife, and I'll leave it at that.

The people I served with can't be measured in friendship. I really have no friends. I have acquaintances, and then I have my brothers. I have buddies that I like hearing from now and then, but that's as far as that goes. For instance, one of our brothers passed away several years ago. My company commander asked if I would have his back during his eulogy, and without hesitation my wife and I were on our way to DC for one of ours. I didn't know him, but he was one of the company commander's top squad leaders. It's simply mutual respect, and most of A/2/502 1966 has it. Growing up you have friends, but there is nothing to compare to the person you were in battle with. Jim Finnerty never made it to the 502nd on his first mission with the 327. He was shot 3 times. I visited him at Valley Forge Military Hospital, where he stayed for over a year.

We tried to write home as much as possible, and Mom saved all the letters that she received from me. One time after a battle, I was directing a CH 47 landing zone (LZ). He was coming in to resupply us and pick up those killed in action. I only had one arm on my glasses, and the blast from his props blew my glasses off. Wayne and I couldn't find them. We already had one incident when a squad leader lost his glasses and was killed because he couldn't see. I was told to take the next chopper out to Nha Trang and get another pair of glasses. There was a MARS station there, and I got to make a call home. Dad was at work, but I did get to talk to Mom for 5 minutes. As I read my letters that I sent home several years ago, I really never said much of how rough things were over there. My aunt would send care packages. One time she sent us a large box of toilet paper because I had mentioned that it was hard to come by.

I was married to my first wife and had two daughters and a son when the war came to an end. I really don't have any recollection of the war ending, other than seeing the North Vietnamese entering Saigon on the news.

My return home was by a civilian plane 707 with no ceremony. Dad, Mom, sister, and brother met me at the PHL airport. It was like I went for a year-long visit somewhere on the planet. No one came to visit for several days. Then at random intervals relatives would show up. That was cool. One day you are in a war, and then you come home. It's kind of weird now that I think about it. I do remember my mom waking me on the couch and almost knocking her out. She shook me, and I reacted as if I was still in 'Nam. She never did that again.

I learned many lessons, first and foremost from Sergeant Richard C. Youngbear telling us that he would never order us to do anything that he wouldn't do himself, and I have lived by that code. American soldiers can be as brutal as any other warriors at any time in history. Anything can be accomplished if you try hard enough. Death is inevitable, but it can be delayed. It is totally up to you how you want to live your life. You control your own destiny.

PTSD is real and affects everyone differently. I choose to live with the demons, but not let them control me. I have no regrets about killing. It was my job. But I have learned over the years that the North Vietnamese and the VC soldiers fought an honorable war that ended in their favor. My biggest fear was getting captured. The worst part was leaving our brothers in the field.

The protesters protest because that's what they believe, good or bad. Saying thank you for your service is a wonderful thing that shows respect for what you have done to keep this the greatest country in the world.

We try to have a reunion every other year, but our ranks are dwindling. Bob Tennent John Pippin, Captain McFadden, Plt. leaders John D Mooneyham and Evan Francis, and Frank Renaud all talk and visit when possible. This year we are expecting 25 from the company to show up at Arlington Cemetery on 9/22, our battalion commander's birthday, where we visit the graves of fallen comrades.

My memories of 'Nam are remembering all of the good soldiers who died. They died with honor and dignity. We say a prayer and plant a flag at the 101st monument, saying their names out loud.

Wayne Leathers was there the day I left Nam in my chopper, taking me back to Phan Rang. Wayne Leathers yelled over the chopper noise to "call his mom and tell her he would be home in 12 days." We saluted, and I said "just another day in the life of a U.S. paratrooper."

John Sutor
U.S. Army

101st Airborne Division
Pennsylvania

Greg R. Harle

My name is Greg R. Harle, and I am the proud son of a decorated World War II veteran, Robert Harle, who served with the 101st Airborne Division, 502nd PIR.

I was born in Jamestown, New York, in November 1946. My father became a cabinet builder, inspector, and plant guard. He was also an artist. My mother worked as a waitress and in department stores and factories as well as being a housewife and mother to two sons and a daughter.

My grandfather served in the Army during World War I. My uncle, father, and father-in-law also served in the Army during World War II. My brother was in the Navy during Vietnam. I received my draft notice for Vietnam and decided to go ahead and enlist to have a better choice of what I wanted to do. I chose the Army because of my grandfather's and father's service.

I left by train for Fort Dix, New Jersey, in January 1966. The weather was cold. I was hospitalized for an upper respiratory infection and later graduated basic training in March. I was sent to Fort Gordon, Georgia, where they assigned me to telephone switchboard installation and operations. I graduated first in my class in June. From there, I was sent to Fort Huachuca, Arizona, for advanced training in a combat area.

I didn't have much trouble adjusting to military life, but missed home and my girl, Jan. The food and physical regimen were okay, as I had always been physically active anyway. I made a few good friends and got married in May 1966 at Fort Gordon. I made lots of friends, and many friendships lasted years after I got out. One of them stood up for me when I got married. Departure for Vietnam was in October 1966 with the 459th Combat Area Signal Battalion on a troop ship. The first month on the ship, we had no communication at all. After we settled in, we wrote almost daily. We received R&R in Tokyo and got one phone call home. There wasn't much free time, but I listened to music when I got the chance and played guitar.

I served in Nhatrang-Tuyhoa and Ninhoa. There were B-52 strikes that came close to us, with air strikes by jets carrying napalm and gunships. I was made the company mail clerk and drove 60 miles one way 6 days a week to pick up mail and supplies. Most of the time, I was by myself. When the Tet Offensive started, I was the only one allowed off the compound.

The worst part for me was being unaware of who the enemy was unless I was being shot at. You learned to count your blessings every day, as you never knew how much time you had left. My greatest fear was not coming back and leaving my wife behind. I later came to realize how lucky I was to come home in one piece, as many did not. After all is said and done, I don't regret going, not at all. I got the chance to see life outside of the United States. There was an adjustment in civilian life changing from days to working nights, but I don't think it really changed me. Even though I feel it didn't change who I am, war can't help but change you. The sights, the sounds, and even the smells stay with you for life. The thing I see with a lot of veterans is the lack of wanting to talk about it. It must be something we try to block out. As for my 101st Airborne Dad who fought during World War II, we have learned more in the last couple of years about his experience than we did our whole lives. He is 94 years old as of this writing.

I got out of the service in January 1969 and flew from Cam Rahn Bay to Japan, then on to Fort Lewis, Washington, and back to my wife again. I only had enough money for airfare to Cleveland, Ohio. So my dad and wife came to pick me up. I was well received by my friends and family. It was good to be back home. To this day, my closest friend is a fellow Vietnam veteran. I am a member of Post 777 with the American Legion.

As for the protesters of any war, you have the right to protest government policies, but not the veterans who serve and sacrifice for your freedom. When people thank me for my service today, I think, "Where was the thanks 50 years ago?" But it's a nice gesture.

Greg R. Harle
Army
New York

> Greg Harle's father, Robert Harle trained and fought with my 101st Airborne father in the 502nd PIR, Regimental Headquarters. Both were radio communicators together in Normandy, Carentan, Holland and at the Battle of the Bulge during World War II. Sadly, Robert Harle passed away in July 2014.
>
> -Jenny La Sala

Alfred R. Jenkins

My name is Alfred R. Jenkins, and I was born in Elizabethtown, Kentucky.

Dad was a farmer, and Mom a homemaker. I have an older sister and two brothers. I have uncles and cousins who all served in the military. Prior to being drafted, I was a truck mechanic. Basic training in Fort Polk, Louisiana, was rough. I hated it. They jammed people through the training with limited contact with family, except for a phone call here and there. They treated criminals better than the soldiers. I did not like the commanding officer.

I did not adapt well to military life. I didn't want to be there. I made some friends, but the physical training was difficult with old barracks and terrible food. I later received training in advanced infantry in Fort Sam Houston, Texas. The treatment there was better in all aspects. My best friend, James McCleary, went at the same time. Just as he finished his last test, he went to sick call and three days later died of blood poisoning and pneumonia.

My service ran from December 21, 1965, to October 28, 1967. I organized convoys and radio contact. The men in convoys were attacked by sniper fire and were helpless. It was difficult talking to them on the radio and hearing the attacks, being unable to do anything as they got shot at. The worst part was having no choice about going to Vietnam and leaving my family. My greatest fear was getting killed or caught as a prisoner of war, but I am proud that I served and have more respect for the American flag after having done so.

I get emotional when people thank me for my service. I'm proud that I served, but I got prostate cancer and a cancer spot on my bladder from radioactive seeds from the war. For those two years served, I had the chance to look at how other people lived, but I also feel that I lost two years of my life. The good memories were of my looking forward to getting out and excited about counting down the days. I remember that it was a sunny day over the beautiful blue China Sea when my airplane departed, taking me out of Vietnam.

I mentioned earlier that my best friend, James McCleary, pictured above on the far left, died before at the end of his training and before being sent to Vietnam. He was born in Carrollton, Missouri, and married Nancy Jo Esgar in 1962. He loved cars, hot rods, and drag racing. He was honest, kind, and a comical guy—a good man. This story is in honor of James whose picture appears above. He left behind his wife and mother and is buried in Evergreen Cemetery in Morris, Illinois. The reason I am telling you this is that, in recent years, I married his widow, Nancy.

I have maintained memberships with the VFW and American Legion.

Alfred R. Jenkins
U.S. Army
Illinois

Sarah L. Blum

My name is Sarah L. Blum, and I am a Vietnam veteran.

I was born in Atlantic City, New Jersey, on December 5, 1939. Father was a jeweler, and Mother a telephone operator. My brother worked for the FAA and later with my father in the jewelry store.

Prior to entering the service, I was a nurse working in the intensive care unit at a hospital in Los Angeles, California (1963–1966). My father served in the signal corps during World War II, and my brother as a crew chief on Army helicopters in Germany during the Cold War. I entered the service in March 1966 and was commissioned as a first lieutenant.

The early days of training were spent at Fort Sam Houston, Texas, for 8 weeks and then a 5-month Operating Room Nursing course at Letterman General Hospital in the Presidio of San Francisco. I adapted well as an Army nurse and served as:

1. Operating Room Nurse, 12th Evacuation Hospital in Cu Chi, Vietnam (January 1967–January 1968).
2. Head Nurse, Orthopedic Ward at Madigan General Hospital (January 1968–September 1968).
3. Evening and Night Nursing Supervisor, Madigan General Hospital (November 1970–February 1971).

The 12th Evacuation Hospital was on the edge of the iron triangle where all the fighting was going on in 1967. We were the largest user of fresh blood in all of Vietnam. We supported the 5th Infantry Battalion, the First Infantry, and both the 82nd and 101st Airborne. There were constant mortar attacks while we worked in surgery.

My father sent me stainless steel forceps from his jewelry shop that we sterilized and used to remove shrapnel from soldiers' eyes at the 12th Evacuation Hospital in Cu Chi, Vietnam, where I served.

There was no time for emotions. I could not show my emotions, or the soldiers who came in wounded thought it meant they were going to die. Initially, I had gut-wrenching emotional reactions of horror and an incredible sadness at the utter destruction of these beautiful young soldiers. I saw the worst of humanity and what war does to hearts, minds, and bodies. There were so many young men with irreparably mutilated and mangled bodies. The constant flow of mass casualties left no time or energy to allow my feelings to flow. I had to shut them down.

I made close friends with other nurses and we leaned on each other for support. I also had a great relationship with the Australian soldiers who ran the phone system. In the middle of the night, when everyone was asleep or on duty, I would crank the phone and ask, "Are you working?" An Aussie voice would answer: "Working." We would talk. He would listen as I spewed out what emotions I had from the day and night. Then I would ask him to tell me about Australia, which allowed me to relax and get some sleep.

My mother wrote letters weekly, and I wrote back. I also had a few Military Area Radio Station (MARS) calls back home. The radio called ham operators, and they relayed the calls to close to home until I connected with home.

For recreation, we mostly went dancing and drinking—that was how I dealt with the emotions I had inside. I danced like a crazy woman.

I came home on a Southwest Airlines plane, my Freedom Bird. When I arrived at Travis AFB in San Francisco, they would not let us off the plane for two hours and told us not to wear our uniforms. It was not what I expected. It was very disappointing, but I was numb.

My friends were kind and supportive upon my return home from Vietnam, and so was my family, but outside that it was hostile toward Vietnam veterans.

I did best when I was still in the Army Nurse Corps working as an Army nurse at an Army hospital. I had a hard time outside that. I was used to dealing with life and death all the time and having intensity. I could not handle women talking about mundane things in life and could not relate to people anymore unless they had been to Vietnam.

I was at the University of Washington in my graduate course when Saigon fell. It was devastating. All the inner protections I put up to keep my emotions in started to crack. No one there understood, even though I was studying psychotherapy. They told me to "get my shit together or get out." I made the wall inside me stronger to keep everything contained.

I was totally changed by my wartime experience and no longer judgmental about other women's choices. I became stronger within myself and had the ability to handle anything coming my way. I trusted myself. Over time I came to understand the effects of war and wounding, the inner conflicts regarding war, and the effects on our earth and the people in Vietnam. I became a specialist in healing PTSD and other wounds of war and developed a deep compassion for others and our world.

Ultimately, with 5 years of therapy, I became strong, clear, authentic, and in touch with myself, my emotions, and the Divine.

Everything changed after Vietnam. I have never been the same. It was a forever changed, and I often tell people it is the gift that goes on giving. It took away my faith, which took years of work to restore, yet my faith and connection to the Divine are stronger and clearer than ever before. Because I had to shut down my feelings in Vietnam, I also had to restore my ability to feel, which took years to do. In that time my turmoil was hurtful to my relationships. I married while my depth of feeling was shut down, and when I reconnected to my inner feelings, I knew my marriage was not working and had to leave. My service in Vietnam also affected my body in a number of ways that had to be healed over time as well. My service in Vietnam was the most intense ongoing experience of my life and taught me about wounding and healing like nothing ever has. It led to me to become a wounded healer with abilities far beyond anything I learned in school.

The good memories of my experience are mostly the esprit de corps we had together at our hospital, saving many lives, and loving my brother and sister service members.

The worst part of the war was the day Johnny came in with the entire bottom of his body desecrated by American artillery. We had to take off his legs all the way up to his hips, and I was standing in his blood for hours, not knowing if we were doing the right thing by saving his life.

War is never okay. War destroys life in all forms. When wounds are not healing, there is a reason. Find that, and healing can take place. Separate the war from the warrior and welcome home our warriors who go in our name, even if you do not agree with why they were sent. Although I became a protester after the war, I do not regret going. The only thing I would say is this: Never attack returning service members, even if you are against the war. I feel proud of my service now, but for many years I did not.

I did veterans work for years and was a member of the board of directors of the Vietnam Veterans of America. I am now connected to many women who served and who were sexually assaulted in the military.

Sarah L. Blum
U.S. Army Nurses Corps
Washington

Sarah has become a great healer and speaker; she is passionate about what she does and lectures about it. This has led her to interview other women veterans and sharing their stories in two books, the first of which is completed and published:
Women Under Fire: Abuse in the Military.
http://womenunderfire.net

Coming Soon: *Women Under Fire: PTSD and Healing*

CHAPTER XII

THE SIMILARITIES OF WAR

Love, Compassion, and PTSD

My father, David Clinton Tharp, was a decorated 101st Airborne paratrooper during World War II. Although he survived the battles of Normandy, Carentan, Holland, and the Battle of the Bulge, combat came with both a physical and mental price, as it does with all soldiers in all wars.

In 1999, my father passed away, and our family went through some of his wartime keepsakes to pay our respects. The most interesting of these keepsakes was a stack of letters he sent home to my mother between 1943 and 1945. I had seen them as a young girl, but I never got past the opening "hello darling" or "sweetheart" without giggling and placing them back in a drawer. Reading them as an adult, I was overwhelmed at the story his writing told.

His Word War II letters, saved for more than 70 years, now offered incredible insights into the young hero who bravely honored his country. The letters were filled with testaments of love for his future wife (my mother) and spoke of his desire to start a family. They exposed a sense of pride, loyalty, and patriotism that resulted from serving his country. The letters also contained something that I was not ready for: Stories of Dad recalling frozen dead soldiers stacked up like corded wood or seeing friends vaporized into thin air were devastating. However, they also offered insights into some of my father's post-war behaviors as well as what he was like before his gentle soul was compromised.

War changes a soldier. It changes his family too. The battle does not end when the troops come home. My father used to say, "We all have our crosses to bear." Dad suffered from severe pain caused by shrapnel, intense night terrors, and a quick temper to an otherwise gentle disposition. These traits had an enormous impact on me as a little girl, but nothing came near the times when Dad would leave with his hunting rifle and threaten suicide. The house became silent. My mother was silent. I didn't move or speak. But he always returned, with everyone acting as though nothing happened.

Only after the passing of my father and publishing his letters in *Comes a Soldier's Whisper* did I fully appreciate both the greatness of my father and the silent struggles he constantly battled. His letters have allowed me to offer greater love and compassion to others impacted by what we now know as Post-Traumatic Stress Disorder (PTSD). Jim knew my father for more than 14 years. They were both veterans of different wars. Each carried his demons, but neither spoke of their experiences. It was after Jim read my father's letters that he brought to my attention the vast similarities of sentiments he related to.

My brother, David Livingston Tharp, who passed away in 2009, and Vietnam veteran ex-husband Jim Markson each presented similar traits upon their return from combat—traits that I now understand. Such has become the impetus for my advocacy in helping our veterans.

Perhaps in understanding our fathers, brothers, mothers, and sisters who serve to protect our country we can begin to understand ourselves a bit more. We wish to share excerpts from stories of other veterans of World War II, Korea, Iraq, and Afghanistan to name just a few and to show the common thread of the war experience as shared by all soldiers and families of all wars.

~Jenny La Sala

BYGONE WARS

In this land of bygone war,
over which vast armies once did roar,
The second generation now has come,
To view what their fathers had supposedly won.

They look perplexed at what they find
A people who once pleaded with body and mind,
Now lower their heads in a sleepy slumber
While that second generation bolsters their numbers

What once was fought for so fiercely,
Is now remembered by few and scarcely.
I ask myself a puzzling question.
Where is my fate my destination?

I've roamed two lands where my countrymen fought and died
And still no answer as for what they strived
If no answer I can find, in my beleaguered weary mind,
I'll turn to God in a hypocritical way, to try to find for what, with their lives they did pay.

~ Jim Markson, July 3, 1968, written about WWII and Vietnam

Leopold J. Martin (World War II)

Dad never spoke of his emotions or of witnessing combat-related casualties or destruction. He never talked about these subjects and only told us of "humorous" events. Dad's greatest fear during his wartime experience was that his mother might receive a KIA (killed in action) letter. As far as him having any regrets for service, I don't think so, as he re-enlisted. He believed in hard work, patriotism, and doing things well. He was proud to have served. He hated the Vietnam protesters.

Dad did not speak of his actual wartime experiences, so I cannot say how the war affected him directly—well, not until an incident when my father was in his 80s and we were at the doctor's office. He started crying to a nurse out of the blue about "all the dead babies." As soon as I heard that, I figured it had to be about his war experience during World War II. He was placed in an assisted living facility in 2008 for his safety. Unlike most of the others there, he never needed a walker. I told Dad that the director there was a colonel. That's all it took! He totally respected and obeyed when the colonel redirected him. He still understood the chain of command after all those years.

~Written by Gary L. Martin about his 101st Airborne father, Leopold J. Martin, who served during World War II
Tennessee

John Sherman (World War II)

It's hard to say how my wartime experiences affected me. I appreciate being alive and being able to function. I know full well that anyone else put in my situation would have done as well or better. I don't have good memories of the war. The worst part was having a fear of what might happen. My greatest fear was being under artillery bombardment. The one lesson I learned from military service was to choose the guys you would like to have on your back in a firefight as friends.

It was an honor to serve this great country. The longer I live, the more I think that we would be speaking German and would have become slaves if we had lost. As for protesters of the war, I have no use for those who protest and simultaneously reap the advantages of the sacrifices of those who served and continue to serve our country. I am always proud when people thank me for my service and let them know how much I appreciate them and their remarks.

We had two sons, but lost our oldest son, Jack, on June 24, 1993, the worst day of my life. Before he passed, I took him to Holland and Bastogne. He died in our arms 8 months later. One of the last things he said to us was that he loved us and the trip to Holland was the best thing that ever happened for him. It was a relief for me because I would not answer many of his questions about the war. I was wrong to do that. When he was hospitalized in Holland, they took wonderful care of him. When I tried to pay the bill for his release, they told me I paid for it back in September 1944. To this day, the Dutch have never forgotten the liberation of their country.

John Sherman
101ˢᵗ Airborne Division

327 Glider Infantry
Oregon

> John Sherman is featured in Kevin Brook's book, *Glider Infantryman: Behind Enemy Lines in World War II.*

Guy C. Whidden, II (World War II)

We knew exactly where we were going, but not what was to become of us.

My story is not the history of a war—its purposes, its conduct, campaigns, defeats, victories, horrors, and outcome. It is the story of experiencing it over a 4-year period of vital growth and development in my life. I make no hero's claim of glory, although it has been a consuming goal enthusiastically pursued. Having reached my sunset years, I have at last found that glory simply by being one of an increasingly rare group of World War II survivors. It is my belief that my frequent letters home are a part of history.

The letters are a human history of one young life among millions who suffered, endured, died, or survived man's inhumanity to man.

Guy C. Whidden, II
101st Airborne Division
502nd PIR
Maryland

Author of *Between the Lines and Beyond, Letters of a 101st Airborne Paratrooper.*
www.guywhidden.com

Doris "Joy" Thurston (World War II WAC)

I was born in Chicago, Illinois, in October 1923 and became a member of the Women's Army Corps (WAC) from 1944 to 1946.

The *Comes a Soldier's Whisper* book cover and website (www.comesasoldierswhisper.com) music brought tears to my eyes. I was a WAC and part of a special project for the Women in Military Service for America Foundation (WIMSA), serving in the hospitals with returning wounded soldiers during World War II.

I knew I was making history, so I recorded my experiences in words and pictures in *A WAC Looks Back: Recollections and Poems of World War II*. My mission in the Army was to lift and inspire hopeless patients, helping them return to civilian life. I had a hard time adjusting back to civilian life and felt like a round peg in a square hole. Drawings and poetry helped me cope. In the end, it was the Army that recognized and used all of my talents of portrait painting, sculpture, and welcoming patients to the hospital. I was referred to as "Miss Reconditioning." Upon leaving the service, I was trying to make up for two lost years of service and later realized that the war deepened my love of art, song, and acting.

I cried uncontrollable tears while writing *A WAC Looks Back* in 1995 and realized that painting the Beatitudes 20 years after her discharge was a form of healing my PTSD. I am proud and grateful for the opportunity to serve. The Army opened up my life to meeting all kinds of people. The world was my friend. I have a deeper love for my country, for man, and for God.

The *Comes a Soldier's Whisper* book cover and website music brought tears to my eyes. The book is a great legacy and helps in healing from PTSD as well.

Doris "Joy" Thurston
Army WAC Veteran/Artist/Author/Performer
Florida

> At the age of 90, Doris remains active with her daily pursuits with the art of giving back. She went on to share her WAC poems and drawings along with the Beatitude paintings with social workers and psychiatrists at the Palm Beach VA. They thought her work should help veterans with PTSD. Additional information regarding her past and present works can be viewed at www.DorisThurstonArts.com
>
> Doris has written several books:
> *A WAC Looks Back: Recollections & Poems of World War II*
> *Stroke! A Daughter's Story: Trauma and Triumphs Caring for A Father with Aphasia*
> *The Temple Within: Sonnets and Asanas*

Vincent J. Riccio (World War II)

My father was a flight engineer and top turret on a B-7 in the 95th bomb group.

I can't say that the wartime experiences of my father, Vincent J. Riccio, impacted my childhood or adult life—except insofar as that knowing the hardships that past generations endured gives me a greater appreciation for the liberties that we enjoy today. It is also hard for me to say how the war changed him, as I didn't know him before his military service. I know he suffered from the cold and claimed that all who survived the Black Hunger March suffer from the cold. He also had an aversion to eating boiled potatoes. After having been a POW, Dad said, "You learn about people, you learn about human nature, you learn what the human body can take. The ones who couldn't take it didn't make it."

I didn't find out that my father had been a prisoner of war in World War II until I was in high school. Even then, he didn't say much. He didn't seem to think it was all that important—in his words, "Not a big deal." Almost 50 years passed before he shared his story with us, and only then after he started having nightmares and flashbacks to his war experiences. His story revealed to me a side of him that I had never known, a glimpse into what he was like as a young soldier: fun-loving, level headed, and resourceful. He chose not to dwell on the negative, instead recognizing the humanity of the people he encountered on both sides of the conflict.

~Candace Riccio Salem
Israel

> Candace has published her father's story in the book *Ever the Patriot: Recollections of Vincent J. Riccio, World War II Veteran and POW.*

Robert Harle (World War II)

Robert Harle of the 101st Airborne, Five-O-Deuce shared England barracks with David C. Tharp, and they fought in D-Day and the Battle of the Bulge together. Here are his comments from our meeting in June 2013.

I fondly remember your Dad as a soft-spoken, handsome, and very tall man, unlike some other rough, "tough cookies" they had in the soldier mix. When you saw your fellow comrades killed, you didn't hesitate, but there were some who went over the edge and continued after a soldier was already gone. I remember a young German soldier had already passed away when a few of our soldiers kept tearing at his uniform and ripped off a flower from his lapel, the country flower, Edelweiss. Many of the German soldiers wore the flower, representing strength and courage. I waited and went back to place the Edelweiss flower back on the soldier's lapel. It just wasn't right. That young man was like me.

The war changed me. But the changes surfaced a few years after the war. I developed a temper and would break out into a rage at the sound of a car backfiring or something as simple as a dog acting up. My wife would sometimes leave the house during those episodes. But I have mellowed over time. I'm 92 years old. There aren't many of us left now.

Robert Harle
101st Airborne Division
502nd PIR
Regimental Headquarters
New York

Such a loving gesture amidst the horrors of war speaks accolades of human kindness and is a tribute to this very special man. It was through emotion and tear-filled eyes that Robert Harle recalled this memory. After all these years, the pain remains. Like Bob, my gentle dad developed quite a temper from the war, which although mellowed with time, wreaked havoc with his otherwise gentle soul.

Mr. Harle passed away on July 19, 2014.

-Jenny Tharp La Sala

Vernon H. Sparks (World War II)

My father didn't do very well with the circumstances for most of his life following World War II.

He brought his mental health disorder home to family and friends. Medical professionals did not know what to do with these men following brief treatment and release from various recovery treatment hospitals around the country. The good news is that it is estimated that only around 10 percent of combat veterans suffered from symptoms of PTSD, but still this is a large number, especially when you consider the number of veterans during the entirety of World War II. Many who suffered extreme anxiety and depression in battle committed suicide according to the Department of Defense records. If you pile on the implications of inter-generational PTSD among spouses and children, the legacy of World War II and later wars lives on from one generation to the next.

I believe the suffering connected to PTSD is so severe and debilitating that it can be worse than death and definitely compares to the suffering that occurs from a severe physical wound.

~Steve Sparks
Retired information technology sales and marketing executive
Oregon

Steve recognizes that the battle fatigue referenced during World War II is known today as Post-Traumatic Stress Disorder, a psychological disorder that develops in some individuals who have had major traumatic experiences. The person is typically numb at first, but later has symptoms including depression, excessive irritability, guilt (for having survived while others died), recurrent nightmares, flashbacks to the traumatic scene, and overreaction to sudden noises. Post-traumatic stress became known as such in the 1970s due to the adjustment issues of some Vietnam veterans. Steve has published his compelling life experience with his Word War II veteran father in *Reconciliation, A Son's Story*.

Thomas R. Galloway (Korea)

KOREA -THE FORGOTTEN WAR- "UNLESS YOU WERE THERE"

My name is Thomas Galloway and I was born on April 2nd 1931 in Oswego, New York.

James Raymond Galloway, my Dad, was a self taught radio and television repairman, while Catherine, my Mother, raised 5 children, two Sister's: Patricia, "Pat;" and Margaret Ann, "Nan"and three boy's: James Raymond, Jr., "Dick;" Tom, "me;" and younger Brother, Robert, "Bob."

Dad served in the Army Air force in France during WWI. My brother James, (Dick) served in the Navy at age 17. He was a bow gunner on the LST 1017 and participated in several Island invasions in the Pacific during WWII. My sister Pat obtained a nursing degree after high school from the Plattsburgh S.T. College. But she worked as a welder on army tanks at the beginning of the war. She then joined the Navy as a Petty Officer. But while on base in Florida, she and several others were struck by a motorcycle. She was discharged after a year in the hospital. My younger brother Robert served in Ft. Knox with the Army Tank corp., as a Corporal. He also served in Korea with the same unit. He was later employed as the Chief Spokesman for 3 court judges in the Hillsborough Court System in Tampa, Florida.

A neighbor and friend who served in WWII in the 82nd Airborne came home in uniform. I never forgot how sharp he looked in that uniform. At that point, I could think of no other branch of the military to join. Three of my high school friends and I enlisted in the Army on February 7, 1951 in Syracuse, New York.

My basic training was at Ft. Campbell, KY and then on to Jump School in Ft. Benning, Georgia. I returned to Ft. Campbell for

Advanced Infantry training and then to Ft. Drum, New York in January, for winter maneuvers. We were in the field for 10 days and nights, with the weather being 20 below zero. We were without heat or winter clothing, except for Parkas. Some of the Companies were assigned to Alaska for training.

Although a bit shy, I was very athletic and fit right into the regimen. I attached myself to a few close friends, and did not mind the food or military life.

I stayed in touch with Mom by writing now and then. I don't know why, but it seemed better, at that time, not to stay so close to my family. But I always loved them very much. I served at Ft. Campbell, Kentucky with E co. 503rd Regt., of the 11th Airborne Division as a Squad Leader.

In early 1952, as volunteer's, several of us were sent to Korea as replacements with the 187th Airborne Regimental Combat Team. This was a special "commando type" unit. It was designed to have lots of "fire power" and be able to move fast in order to assist other units that may be in trouble.

While with Co., "G" 187th A.R.C.T., I witnessed close in-air strikes by Navy Corsairs. There were lots of scary and harassing night patrols with our Police dogs. We listened to the enemy via our "Mike's," that we planted at the water holes, during nighttime. We came under heavy artillery shelling and mortar fire several times. I was lucky not to get hit, but some others did. After several of our troops were killed and wounded, we would see them in the body bags waiting to be shipped home. But we never really talked much about it. It seemed like if we did not mention it, we would be safe! Now I wonder, why?

We went back to Camp Wood, in Kumamoto, Japan, for Airborne training, and Parachute Jumps. Several Airborne Military Policemen were lost in Korea, and we were asked if anyone would like to volunteer to be trained as a replacement M.P., and I thought that when I finally got home, I would like to be a NYS Trooper, so I volunteered for an interview, and three of us were accepted.

We later received M.P. Training by the Japanese Logistical Command, (JLC), the regular Army Soldier's, who ran Camp Wood. Later on I returned to Korea as an M. P. with the 187th Airborne Regimental Combat Team. Things went fairly well for several months, and while on our second tour in Korea a truce was signed at Panmunjon.

Around the same time, I was on Military Police night patrol in the mountains with my Sergeant, Andy Leon, from Arizona, and we came upon someone who was heavily armed and walking the roads in the dark. Since everyone was still armed, we did not think too much about it! I was driving, and Andy said, "pull over while I check him, and if everything is alright we will give him a ride." So I pulled up with the Trooper on the passenger side. Andy stepped out of the vehicle, and asked, "Where are you going?" and, without provocation the soldier turned and at point blank range, shot Andy in the stomach, and quickly shot me in the shoulder.

He blew me right out of the jeep, and onto the road, and I landed on my stomach. He then put the barrel of the rifle to my Sergeant's head who was still alive, and while Andy pleaded for his life, he shot him between the eye's and killed him.

The Jeep was in neutral, and rolled back about 30 feet, and tipped sideways into a small ditch. The headlights shone on us like a lit up stage, while everything else was pitch dark as it was around 2 p.m., and we were fairly high up in the mountains.

While on the ground, I reached for my 45 pistol, but felt my finger go into the bottom of the weapon. Somehow the clip fell out and I was now unarmed, so I lay real quite like I was dead. I heard him run, out of the glare of the headlights, and then heard him stop and slowly walk back towards me, on the gravel road.

He stopped over me, and said, "hey, hey you!" With my face down from him, I almost said help, but remembered Andy asking him not to kill him, so I kept quiet, and prayed.

At that point, he put his M1 rifle under my right side, and tried to roll me over, and I grabbed the barrel with my left hand, and he was so surprised that he jumped backwards so hard that he pulled me to my feet.

While I held the barrel of the gun, and kept moving left and right, so he could not shoot me, he fired again, and his second shot missed me, as it went right between my legs and into the road. At this point, I was getting weak from loss of blood, and as we wrestled for the rifle, I decided that if I was going to die, he was coming with me. So I grabbed him by the arm, and ran off the side of the cliff in the dark, and kept struggling with him. We landed about 20' down the hill. He kept trying to rub dirt and gravel in my face and eyes, but I eventually overcame him, and knocked him out, with a soft-ball size rock. I fractured his skull.

With my belt flashlight, I took his name off of his fatigues, and then I crawled on my hands and knees up the hill, back into the headlight glare. I retrieved the murder weapon, as I knew it had his serial number on it, and then checked Andy, to make sure he was not alive.

I had to walk some distance in the dark for help. I was getting weaker, and was bleeding severely. Just then a South Korean truck came towards me in the dark, and I stopped them, with the killer's confiscated rifle. They held me on the running board, and turned around to take me back to the M.P. station. They saved my life!

Our M.P.s found the killer unconscious, and captured him. Our Criminal Investigation Division later found out that he was going to "K" Company with the intention of killing the First Sergeant and several others. I never found out why.

The worst part for me was when I was in a Mash Hospital Tent, and had to tell the Red Cross Lady what to say when notifying my parents that I was wounded but would be okay. Around that same time, I received a "Dear John" letter from my old High School girlfriend. That was a pretty low time for me, lying in bed thinking about all of this.

Also, I was trying not to think about how the news of my Sgt., Andy Leon, getting killed, after 12 years in the Airborne, would affect his wife and two kids back home in Arizona. It was a pretty sad time!

The nice thing was that General William Westmoreland, our leader, came to the MASH Hospital Tent, to visit the wounded, and actually sat on my bed and asked me to tell him what happened. He told me that he was putting me in for the Soldier's Medal, for Heroism!

I did receive the Medal, authorized by President Eisenhower, after I was home for about 8 months.

Years later I was notified by Governor Patacki's Office, in Albany, NY that I would be receiving the NYS Conspicious Service Cross, for the same action. My family got to see that presentation, and it made me feel very good. It seems like it was yesterday!

Usually, my greatest fear was that I would not be good enough to make my family proud of me. I never to this day had any regrets about going.

A military friend, a Pathfinder, from Ft. Campbell, Tom Henderson and I stayed in touch for many years. He actually ended up marrying a showgirl, from Vegas, and working on the space program in California.

Another friend from my squad at Ft. Campbell was Bob McCarthy who left several months ahead of me for Korea. We heard that he got shot and died. I never heard anymore. But many years later, I received a telephone call asking if I was the Tom Galloway that was in the Paratroopers. I said "yes." The caller said, "This is your old friend, Bob McCarthy." I said, "It can't be, as he's dead" to which he said, "He's talking to you, you A..H.." and laughed.

Bob had been shot 6 times by a Chinese soldier with a Burp Gun, and lived. He was in the hospital in Japan for a year and then in another hospital in Massachusetts for another year. Bob is now retired in Vero Beach, Florida and married to a very nice English girl, Brenda, and they have two grown children. He served 12 years in the Florida Attorney General's office as a criminal investigator. He later developed the "Island Hopper" boats in the Miami area with attached Parachutes as seen on television. The tourist's loved them. He later sold the company for a bundle. Bob is legally blind now but leads an active life. He calls me at least once or twice a week, and I have visited him in Vero Beach after over 62 years. It's simply amazing.

While we were in Camp Wood in Japan, we spent time on pass in Kumamoto, Japan, a large and interesting city. They loved the 187th Airborne, and called us "Rakkasans." It loosely means, in Japanese, "men in falling down umbrellas."

I returned home during the Christmas week of 1953. We left Yokohama Japan, by ship, along with hundreds of other soldiers, and Marines. We spent Christmas Day onboard ship. I received a good welcome home and reception from family and old friends, many whom were veterans returning home at the same time.

I had a difficult time adjusting to a non-military life of effectiveness and discipline. I met a beautiful girl, Bridget Mahunik, and got married. We had a child and I then entered S.U.N.Y., Oswego, to become a H.S. Teacher of Industrial Arts, and Technology. After 10 years. I left Teaching to enter the Real Estate field, as a land and home developer. Many other veterans attended at the same time. Later on, we had 3 more Children.

I have met or heard from several close military friends over the years. They are very special to me and always will be. I have been a Life member of the American Legion, VFW and Disabled Vets for over 55 years. I'm very proud of belonging for so long.

In honor of veterans of all wars and together with another retired veteran of the Air Force, we presented to the Oswego, N.Y. City Council and Mayor, a program to re-tree the main street of Oswego, from city limit to city- limit for about 4 or 5 miles. They agreed and we now have several hundred trees purchased by citizens with a bronze plaque at the base of the tree recognizing a veteran. This program is very popular, and called "Tree's for Vets." On Memorial Day, and Veterans Day, yellow ribbons decorate the trees.

I honestly believe that the military service greatly enhanced my life, for the better. The discipline stayed with me right to this day. I believe that I have benefitted greatly from this. I would have made many more mistakes, if not for the training we received in the Airborne. I would not be alive today, except for my military training! Always give 110% to anything that you commit to do. Never lie or cheat, and you will always feel good about yourself!

For those who protest the war, I say that it's because of what we and the veterans ahead of us did and continue to do today that allows you to think and act the way you do. That's America, and I'm damn proud of her.

I was walking behind a young military couple and their child recently, at the Syracuse Airport, and I had my 187th Airborne baseball cap on, and was thinking how young they looked. Just as they turned the corner, he looked right at me and said, "Thank you sir for your service." It stunned me and brought tears to my eyes… I said, "No, I thank both of you for what you are doing now!" What a great country we live in!

I know that the Korean Conflict is often referred to as "the forgotten war" but not to me or to the thousands of young men that were there. Let's not forget that around 36,000 Americans lost their lives during the 37 months in Korea. More than 100,000 were wounded with 8,177 MIA.

My awards include entitlement to The Soldiers Medal, The Combat Infantry Badge, Senior Parachutist Wings, Korean Campaign Ribbons with 4 battle stars, The Presidential Unit Citation, United Nations Service Ribbon and The Good Conduct Ribbon, and the NYS Conspicious Service Cross.

From my own experience, I honor and respect all veterans.

Thomas R. Galloway
187th Airborne Regimental Combat Team
Infantry and Military Police Detachment.
New York

Well I never knew that going back in my mind like this would be so enlightening. I am grateful for this opportunity.

Lisa Parrott (Iraq)

I was born in 1977 in the outskirts of Newark, Ohio. My name is Lisa Parrott. I grew up on a small farm before moving into the city for middle and high school.

My mother was an elementary physical education teacher and my father has been in the automotive industry his entire career. I have two siblings, a younger brother (by 2 years) and younger sister (by 11 years).

Before joining the service I was attending college at Denison University, working on a psychology degree. My grandfather served in World War II and my uncle served as well although I'm not sure during what period.

I enlisted as a reservist in the Marine Corps at the start of my junior year, and transitioned to the officer program before going to OCS the summer before my senior year. Because of this I did not attend boot camp and was commissioned after graduating. I enlisted to make some extra money while in college, and to get self-defense training. I joined the Marine Corps because it's the best, and I enjoy a challenge.

I left for Officer Candidate School the summer of 1998 to attend the 10 week training with Alpha class. After completing the program I returned home to complete my senior year at college. Upon graduation and commissioning in May 1999, I left to attend The Basic School with Echo Company. From there I was selected to become a supply officer and headed to Ground Supply Officer Course in Feb 2000.

I've completed SERE with the cold weather mountain training in Bangor, ME, Cold Weather training at Bridgeport, CA, Defense Equal Opportunity Management Institute in Cocoa Beach, FL and a handful of budgeting and supply classes.

Adapting to military life was a challenge initially as I pushed my body beyond physical barriers I thought possible. The food was amazing – simply because I felt like I was always starving. The social life was very different; it becomes almost incestuous in a way. While stationed on Hawaii the amount of people I could hang out with was very limited, as you can't fraternize with certain ranks no matter who you are. It's hard to connect and associate with civilians so most of your friends are from your unit and in the military.

I started my career at Cherry Point, NC as the Supply Officer for MAG-14, the largest air group in the Marine Corps. From there I became the Base Property Officer for Kaneohe Bay, HI and then relocated to Camp Pendleton, CA as the Supply Officer for the 15th Marine Expeditionary Unit (MEU).

During my career I participated in Ulchi Focus Lens in South Korea, and two deployments with the 15th MEU. During the first deployment we entered Iraq as part of the surplus and our base was rocketed. I supported combat teams by going into the city as a female searcher. On the second deployment I ran the logistics efforts for Infinite Moonlight in Jordan.

The hardest part about combat is wondering when it's going to be you next. Sometimes it feels like the worst lottery around, chance and luck play so much into your opportunity for survival. Seeing good people struck down by random events is frustrating, because there is very little you can do about it most of the time. Coming back is even worse – seeing how much people take the US and life for granted is difficult, and a bigger cause of depression and PTSD than I think we realize.

Being a member of the military gives you an automatic in with me. I know we share similar values, mission and dedication to our country. I know you have been to hell and back, so we often can bond on those memories quicker than people I've known for years. My best friends have all served, I think it's hard to understand who I am or what I believe in if you haven't.

Email was a blessing during my deployments and made communicating with friends and family easy. I would often make monthly or 'special reason' phone calls also. The only challenge to making calls was finding an available phone in a quiet location. Often phone hubs could get loud, and difficult to hear. They could get expensive too, so it was good to have a few phone cards available in case you ran out of time. It was always exciting to get real letters and care packages. In remote locations like Iraq having someone ship you simple things like shampoo, conditioner and tampons made your day. Getting the chance to make a choice in those purchases was even better! I would email my mom a list of nice to have items (like my preferred lotion) and she would send out a care package as often as I needed. That could make your week!

I love playing rugby, and was able to do so while in the military most of the time. I met amazing female civilian friends through rugby. It was hard to make practices though, so eventually I stopped playing for a regular team and just played when I could attend a game. I also started hashing while in California, and was able to run a hash in Singapore and Australia, which was an exciting opportunity.

I was living in Seattle when Osama bin Laden was killed. At the time I was preparing to move to San Diego to join my deployed other half. I had already left the military by the time Iraq ended and moved into Operation New Dawn.

During the first 15th MEU deployment I asked my parents to join me for the tiger cruise portion of our return from Iraq. My dad agreed, and we had to repeatedly adjust the dates as our deployment was extended twice (for a total of 3 extra months). He was able to meet me in Hawaii and completed the trip back to San Diego with me via ship. My family then flew out to San Diego to meet us. On my return from the second deployment I flew out of Hawaii to Ohio to see my family and return to San Diego with my dogs. During both deployments my parents watched my dogs.

My family was excited to see me return home from both deployments. I had a number of awesome friends in San Diego who also gave me a great send off and welcome home. The best part was coming back in time to celebrate my 30th birthday party with best friends from rugby and the Marine Corps. The external community in San Diego was less welcoming, and I ended up getting in a fight with a young immature kid who called the military baby killers and said he wished he wasn't an American. That was my first real confrontation with PTSD and the anger issues that would continue to chase me for years.

Adjusting to civilian life wasn't too bad after coming home, other than getting used to handling anger and how much people take our country and their opportunities for granted. It's frustrating to not be able to solve the problems in our country. I get upset seeing how entitled people in government (with power) and those with money treat our country in such a manner. Having people screw with our benefits is scary, and the horrible inefficiency in the VA is appalling.

War changed my perspective and the way I look at the world. I have a deep love of anyone who serves in the military and the families that support them.

After leaving the military I moved to Seattle to be closer to a best friend I met while in the Marines. While living there I met my other half, who is currently an active duty Marine. Staying close to the military in that regard has been a blessing and a curse. When he deploys I remember how much I loved the chance to participate in the big game, and have developed great respect for those family members at home.

I've stayed connected to the Veteran community through work by joining Amazon's military recruiting team. I have also coached Veterans throughout their transition and am completing a dissertation for my PhD on the subject of transition challenges. As a Mission Continues Fellow I was able to do a lot of satisfying work with other Post 9/11 service men and women. I'm connected to multiple Veteran organizations and stay in touch with Veterans across the world through social media.

Wartime made me a better person, by teaching me more about the world and the challenges that exist out there for others. Being a part of the 9/11 era also connected me to other amazing individuals who volunteered to support and protect our country. Joining the military is similar to signing up for an athletic sport. Training (such as boot camp) is part of preparing to play your sport, and you get better the more you do. I joined during peacetime and as much as we would have preferred to avoid conflicts, I was able to participate in the big game.

I learned there are more important things in life than my own view of the world. Joining the military gave me a chance to see and do more, as well as enhance my own acceptance of others. One fun lesson was finding out my love of traveling, which also allowed me to build tolerance for the actions of others. Understanding the culture of another country has allowed me to grow as an individual.

The camaraderie during deployments is amazing. It becomes a surreal microcosm where only the people next to you matter, and the problems back home become less important. It's a great way for people to zone out of life and focus only on the mission and survival. Because of this, you become very close to your team. The bond is unlike traditional civilian experiences, and is comparable to the intense pain and suffering during training evolutions (like OCS, TBS, SERE, etc).

Leaving the military was a very difficult decision for me. I felt like I was letting down the Marines who were still in. It was challenging to be in an organization where I didn't get a chance to establish a routine in my life. I struggled building long lasting relationships with boyfriends due to relocations and deployments. My body was also failing in many ways and the military refused to allow me to slow down long enough to get serious injuries corrected. I've been diagnosed with osteoarthritis in both ankles at 36, making walking and running difficult. It would have been impossible to continue training at the same level and complete another 10 years to retirement.

My greatest fear was not being a good enough leader and losing someone that relies on me as a result. I was always afraid I couldn't protect the Marines that worked with me.

As a result of my wartime experience, I have become intolerant of others who spread hate, fear or exert control over the weak and kind. My temper is short, and can often explode when someone takes life or freedom for granted. I've never forgotten those we lost, and continue to lose. It has given me a different perspective on appreciating life and the choices we have in the US. After returning from Afghanistan my other half was unable to go into the supermarket to buy a box of cereal because there were too many to choose from. And yet I've heard people complain that they don't have enough or not the specific kind they want. Sigh.

I do not regret serving, not a chance. I wanted to deploy more. I do occasionally regret not staying in the service longer. If more could be done to eliminate the bad leaders and poor performers I would have enjoyed staying. Sadly with the choices being made by our government I'm glad I left the military, as I'd be terrified about my future job and benefits security.

As far as having anything to say to protestors, I guess I have to say, what protestors? You're never going to get everyone to agree with you or what you're doing, but I know that I fought for his or her right to make a statement. I don't always agree with what they're saying and get very frustrated that some choose to spread hate, but in the end I support the right to free speech. However, saying it directly to me might trigger an episode of PTSD and uncontrollable anger. I think many protestors are often ignorant individuals who are too cowardly to make efforts to understand the other side.

When people thank me for my service, I don't know that I ever did enough. I will often thank them for thinking of me, but would prefer they recognize those still out there fighting for their country. I'm one of the lucky ones who made it back safely and am no longer being asked to risk my life.

Lisa Parrott
Marine Corps
Washington

Damon Rosenberger (Egypt)

Both my parents served in the U.S. Navy.

My grandfather on my dad's side served in the Navy during World War II and my great grandfather in the Army during World War I. Two uncles on my mom's side served, one in the Navy and the other in all the branches. My oldest brother served in the Army. An uncle served in the Marines, and a cousin served in the Navy. My parents have passed away. I have two older brothers. Dad never did talk about his service. The time I did sit down with my father, he refused to talk about his time in Vietnam.

From a very young age I always knew I wanted to join the Army and serve with the 101st. With all of the Navy veterans in my family, you would think I would have joined the Navy, but being out at sea for months on end wasn't for me. I joined the Army in December 1990 to go to the first Iraq war. All my friends thought I was nuts! But the war ended before I got to leave for basic training. There were multiple drill instructors in your face all the time. I joined the Army to be an 11 Bravo Infantrymen. Training consisted of ground warfare.

Adapting to military life wasn't really that hard, but it took a while to get used to the physical demands of the unit I was assigned to. It was nothing like basic training and AIT. Barracks life wasn't that bad. I stayed in touch with family and friends back home with the good 'ole pen and paper or the occasional phone call.

I never got to see or experience combat, but the training has still had an effect on my life. My battalion was deployed to the Sinai Peninsula, Sharm El-Shaykh, Egypt for the Multinational Force and Observers (MFO). Our mission was to observe the peace treaty between Egypt and Israel. I sometimes wonder what would have happened if the peace treaty had been broken. Well, I know all hell would have broken out. There were some locals who didn't want us there. Plus there were people from other Middle Eastern countries around the area who downright hated Americans! So we were told to be aware of our surroundings at all times if we left the base camp. Plus, we could never go alone. At times it was very stressful. But all the training and all the drills kept us prepared. I always think about what I would do if our country were to ever be invaded—defensive positions, armament, supplies, and things like that. Military training taught me how to endure certain weather conditions and activities. It doesn't matter if it's been 20+ years, my mindset has always been the same.

I later received a medical discharge due to an injury received during a training exercise. I was deployed in Egypt from August 1992 to February 1993. My family was happy to have me home, but readjusting to civilian life was very hard. The first couple of years were the worst. Learning a new way of life and not having the stability I once had were awful. My greatest fear was not being able to live up to my family's military heritage, letting the men to my right and left down. The worst part was having to leave the military and not being able to retire. This was and is the worst thing for me. But I learned from my military experience that freedom isn't free! I do not regret going and would do it all over again, if I could. I have reconnected with old Army buddies, thanks to Facebook.

The men I had the pleasure of serving with—to this day I consider them my brothers! From all the road marches to endless days out in the field, living in the constant rain or heat or cold, looking into their eyes and knowing that they have my back and I have theirs, is a friendship I am glad I have made!

When I encounter protesters of war, I respond by saying, "Yes, you're welcome!" Even though they didn't ask me to join the military and defend their rights, I still did it. When, on the other hand, people thank me for my service, I feel appreciated! I joined of my own free will and didn't do it for the recognition.

Damon S. Rosenberger
101st Airborne Division (Air Assault) 2nd platoon C Company 2nd Battalion 502nd Infantry Regiment
Iowa

Penelope Friedman (Afghanistan)

I had a soldier die before I left for Iraq. He was to be my replacement. I couldn't talk to call or talk to his wife. I wrote her a personal sympathy card. They had a baby together. He was maybe a year old. Everyone grieves in a different way. I have done many funeral details in my time, but to actually have it be your soldier—no words can describe it.

My friendships were earned by trust. The life lessons learned through my military service have given me lasting memories with people from all walks of life offering skills to be shared by all. My greatest fear was not coming home alive. The worst part was not being treated equal. I do not regret going, as I always wanted to know how I would do in a real situation. I'm glad to have served my country.

Readjustment to "normal life," without being in Iraq any longer, was fine. But all of the silly things back home seemed to bother me. Why worry about such small things?

Penelope Friedman
Retired U.S. Army 1987–2011
Former 88 Master Sergeant
Military Intelligence Reserve Command (MIRC)
New York

> Penelope "Penny" Friedman is married to Joe Friedman. They are both retired from military career sand now raising their beautiful daughter.

Joseph Friedman (Iraq)

My mom was very unhappy when I told her I joined the Army! She didn't see the Army, or military service in general, as good enough for me. She of course changed her mind as I was a lieutenant colonel when I retired.

Friendships were formed and camaraderie of service with hundreds from every assignment and all over the world! There is nothing in the civilian world like the camaraderie of those you serve with. I entered active duty in January 1987. I served in Iraq and Kuwait from November 2004 to September 2005. Although we saw no direct combat, we got mortared on a fairly regular basis. But you get used to it.

I had a nice homecoming, to my wife and daughter, who was 11 months old and didn't recognize me! I still had about a year and a half before retirement, but began to make the transition upon my return. How did wartime experiences affect my life? In so many ways it could fill a book! But I wouldn't trade those experiences for anything. I was able to retire knowing that I did my part and learned many life lessons from military service.

My readjustment back to civilian life from the war was no problem. The big adjustment was from 20 years of service to full-time civilian. That was an adjustment that evolved over several years. I still dream of being in the Army virtually every night.

I am proud of my military service to my country.

Joseph Friedman
Former Lieutenant Colonel
Retired U.S. Army
New York

Ronnie Shinault (Iraq and Afghanistan)

My name is Ronnie Shinault, and I'm a veteran of Iraq and Afghanistan.

I was born in Aurora, Illinois, in May 1986. Both of my grandfathers are Vietnam veterans. My mother worked as a waitress, and my father was a roofer. I have a brother and sister, David and Melissa.

I initially set out to play football in college, but lost out on the scholarship, so I enlisted after high school. I attended boot camp in Fort Benning, Georgia, and afterwards completed Advanced Infantry Training in Fort Polk, Louisiana. I was nervous going into the service. No one explained what it would be like. I found it to be difficult and a huge shock, different than any other experience. There were times when I didn't feel that I would survive it.

The physical aspect was not bad and was sort of like the two-day football practices that I used to attend. The mental stress and lack of sleep were difficult and overwhelming, but I loved the barracks experience. It was like a college dorm and having lots of fun socializing with 35 brothers. If you received a letter, it was at least 2 weeks old. All communications were screened. No phones were used, only in dire circumstances. It was not accessible. In our off-duty time, when there was any, we would clean our rifles, play poker, or play football once in a while. There was no access to technology accept a radio to listen to music.

My tours included 13.5 months in Kirkurk, Iraq, 13 months and 18 days in Kandahar, Afghanistan, and the last 6 months in Baghdad. I was a rifleman and squad leader who was responsible for search and seizure of high priority targets taken by force if in conflict. But the main job was to take alive and detain the unit. We were the first wave infantry aimed at setting up a frontline operations base in the middle of the desert and clearing out all Taliban living in the trenches. What started out as fear became a form of numbness after a while. It was part of the job, and going numb kept you alive. It's hard to imagine one can get to that point.

The good memories are only of the travel experiences and companionship of my comrades. The military taught me to not take anything for granted and to think before making choices. It was a life-changing experience in terms of my work ethics, goal setting, and a new appreciation for life, with a strength and desire to live through difficult situations.

I formed a friendship with Tremaine. We went through boot camps and two tours together. He is still alive and in contact with me, but I haven't seen him in 6 years. I've lost contact with the rest of the unit. I don't have a membership to any veterans organization. I do not feel that they are set up to meet the needs of veterans.

The worst part of the war experience was seeing people die and not being able to do anything about it. It was tough making difficult decisions, knowing that outcome might not be positive for all. My greatest fear initially was dying, but after a while, it was the fear of making a mistake that would result in someone else dying.

It took about 6 weeks to transition back home to the States for a debriefing in Fort Drum, New York. I was a wreck and needed to shut my instincts down. My first reaction was violence. That's how they make you human again. I am still adjusting after several years and often experience stress and anger with my body going rigid. Sometimes I will stare without seeing. There are times I have bad dreams calling out coordinates, holding my gun ready for action, and waking up confused.

When I finally returned back home to family, it was nothing major. But my parents had told my brother, who is 8 years younger than me, that I had been away working a lot of hours. I was asked not to tell him where I had been.

For those protesting the war, I would say, "Stop." If we didn't fight or serve, you would not have the freedom to protest in the first place. You would get shot for saying anything in another country. Get on with your life to pursue a worthwhile cause.

People in general do not usually thank us for our service. It is the older people who tend to thank us more. But I do not regret going and am glad that I served.

Ronnie Shinault
Army
Illinois

Jennifer Clark (Afghanistan)

As we talked with the chaplain, he began to relate to us, and what we'd been through on a very real level, speaking from his own experience in the past, which helped comfort us. "You should expect it to be hard going home and re-entering into your old lives. No one back home will have a clue about what you've been through and what you've seen and therefore will likely not be of much help," he warned us.

The chaplain went on to tell me that I would have the most challenge coping as I transitioned back to my work life. No one that I worked with back in the states had any idea what I went through and when I returned they would be expecting the same Lt. Clark that left six months ago. I could tell by my first reaction, to my first day out of the chaos of the firebase, it would be a slow process to get over everything and get re-integrated into my normal life, but I hoped I would continue to go about it in a healthy way and would lean on my support system. I knew that as time passed the hurt would continue to surface as things became more and more "normal". I prayed for the strength to get through it all.

But I had mastered the art of avoidance, keeping all of my pain at arm's length by dodging anything that reminded me of what I had been through. But one night I realized I was in serious trouble. After fourteen months of suppressing any emotion that reminded me of that horrible time, I finally reached the point of no return. I rolled over in bed, exhausted from the previous two sleepless nights. I looked up at my alarm clock and saw it was 12:00 am. My tiny newborn daughter was screaming in hunger from her bassinet at the foot of my bed. I dragged my tired body of out bed and picked up Ayla and cradled her in my arms. My new angel was such an amazing little person already, and I was so grateful to have her in my life. She was my whole world; my love for her was incredible. I knew this love would make all the hurt I was trying so desperately not to feel go away. It had to. I had come to where I didn't know what else to do to avoid going "there", and she had become my reason to move on.

I wanted to do everything by the books, and be the best mom I could for her, so I was adamant about breastfeeding. She was born three weeks early, and we had struggled with this in the hospital, but I was determined. I sat down with her in my bed and began to try to feed her. She continued to cry.

"Ok, Jenn...be patient, you can do this," I told myself, "Remember the different methods they taught you in the hospital." I thought about the endless piles of paperwork they gave me when they discharged us two days before and tried to use the recommendations. Unfortunately, I had no luck. Her screams became louder.

I have to do this! I thought. Why can't she just do what the books say? I felt my emotions bubbling under the surface; a situation that had become such a norm for me over the last several months since I returned from Afghanistan. I had mastered the art of avoidance; keeping all of my pain at arm's length by dodging anything that reminded me of what I had been through.

Now she was screaming. Oh my God, I don't know what the hell to do! I was losing my composure. I looked at the clock again, 2:00am. Two hours had disappeared into the night and I was still in the same place I was when we started. Her screams became louder and her little voice was becoming hoarse.

My Physician Assistant instincts kicked in. What if she is dehydrated? I thought. I reached down and put my finger on her tongue; it was dry. Oh, my God! She is! I looked down at her with concern... but I didn't see Ayla. I was holding that baby - the dying baby in Afghanistan. Her brother had carried her into my clinic in what looked like a potato sack draped over his shoulder, plopped her down on my gurney and untied his sack. I looked inside and saw the skin and bones of what used to be a healthy baby girl, now minutes from death. There was nothing that I could do to save her. As I looked down at my daughter I was right back there in that horrible place. I could smell the filth in the air and I could hear the breath slowly leaving the baby girl's tiny, dying body. I snapped. "Greg! Wake up!" I screamed at my husband, as he lay next to me completely oblivious to my rapid descent into panic. "What is it, Jenn? What's wrong? Is Ayla ok?" He jumped out of bed braced for the worst. "She's starving! I can't feed her! She's dehydrated, look at her!" I screamed. "Calm down, sweetie. It's okay," he tried.

"No! It's not ok! Please! Do something! Please Greg! Go to the store and buy some formula, look at her!" I pleaded. "She's ok, don't worry! Remember they gave us some samples at the hospital? I'll go fix a bottle." He rushed to the kitchen and returned shortly with a bottle in hand. "Here, I'll take her," he said, and finally our screaming baby was content.

Alone in bed, I began to cry. I realized what had just happened, my first flashback. This thing was real. I was not ok. I was damaged goods, and I didn't know how to fix it. I knew the deployment would change me, but I had no idea that this is who would come back from it. Who had I become? The once joyful, funny, optimistic person who had everything under control was lost and nowhere to be found; instead this damaged, emotional wreck had taken over.

I thought about Ayla. Her name had been predetermined for many years; Ayla, after a strong female character in the novel <u>Clan of the Cave Bear</u> that was passed down through the generations of women in my family. The story illustrated a young lady, who despite all odds grew into an amazing woman of strength and character. Her middle name Lee was in honor of my grandmother who was such an influence for me growing up. I had thought I was going to be that strong influence for my daughter, but now I had no idea who I was anymore. My little girl would never know who I once had been. I knew the deployment would be a major part of my life, so I kept a journal to document that time in my life for my future children. Now that child was here; what would she think of her mother?

How had I come to this point? I thought of the journal. It held the key to who I was and who I had become. It was the story of how my life changed forever due to the most traumatic experience I'd ever endured. That night I knew what I had to do…I had to relive it, in its entirety, if I had any hope of rescuing the lost soul inside of me.

Jennifer Clark
Former Air Force Physician Assistant
Florida

> Jennifer Clark has published her journal kept during her deployment taking care of local Afghan people and our soldiers with unimaginable ailments in the book *166 Days: My Journey Through The Darkness*. During her deployment, she discovered that children never had a childhood and women lived in constant fear with men who knew nothing but a life of fighting. The book is both inspirational and motivational—a must read.

Robin R. Findlay (Iraq)

My name is Robin R Findlay and I was born in February 1984 in Streator, Illinois.

My mother is a retired corrections officer. I have 2 half-sisters, Kelly and Erica. I joined the Army right out of high school and took summer college classes, shipping out in September. Ever since I was a young boy, I always had the urge to be a soldier. My grandfather on my father's side served in World War II with the U.S. Army.

The departure for basic training and the early days of training were a nerve-wracking experience. I went from the MEPS station to the airport. We flew from O'Hare Airport in Chicago to St. Louis, Missouri. Then from there we were bused to Ft. Leonard Wood. Upon arrival, I was sweating bullets. All I could think about was "Full Metal Jacket" and just the general stories about drill instructors. As we departed the bus, I immediately got a boot to my chest. Then I was told to get up and do push-ups. Since I was on my back from getting knocked down and being screamed at from all directions, I went to stand because I was confused. Then I got a boot to my stomach, which caused me to kneel down. Now I was in the proper position for push-ups. The early days of basic were pretty much getting smoked and screamed at. Despite all of that, I actually loved basic training. I loved the atmosphere, the training, even the drill sergeants.

Besides my initial training, I also went to Air Assault School, where I learned to repel out of helicopters. In addition to combat training, I also took leadership courses.

I have always been a skinny guy, so the military physical regimen bulked me up with muscle. I always thought I was meant to be the skinny twig while I was growing up, but with basic training and AIT, I found out I could have muscles. I was very proud of my physical fitness once I became acquainted with the military lifestyle. I managed to go from 130 pounds in high school to almost 200 by my second deployment. I was happy I went from looking like a skinny kid to a filled-out man.

I really enjoyed the barracks setup in training. In our downtime, I started talking to my roommates and I didn't realize it then, but I ended up with lifelong friends. It was the same thing with my unit and deployments. I never minded the food. In training, you don't really get time to taste anything anyway. The social life was another unexpected development. I was always a keep-to-myself kind of guy. I had my friends growing up, but this was a whole different animal. I became friends with guys from totally different walks of life, and I really loved that we all got close enough to where we could trust each other with our lives. That's a true friendship when you know the guys to your left and right not only have your back, but also would take a bullet or jump on a grenade. And I would do the same for them.

I did my training at Ft. Leonard Wood, Missouri, and the bulk of my active duty time with the 101st Airborne at Ft. Campbell, Kentucky. I was extremely excited and proud to be a part of that.

I have seen quite a bit of action between my 2 deployments. I witnessed suicide bombers and local Iraqis being shot by their own people. Out of all the unimaginable madness that I have seen, one particular scenario haunts me to this day. Iraqi men were strapping bombs to their young children and telling the children to give soldiers hugs. Once in the hug, the fathers set off the bombs. My squad and I were in a small village near Baghdad. We had reports that this village was going be the destination for a supply convoy ambush, so we were sent to check out the area and investigate. We were walking around the marketplace, and I saw a young child running toward me. We had already been told about the bombs being strapped to them. This boy was running full sprint toward me. Thinking that he had a bomb, I yelled for my squad to get behind the closest building. All of this happened in a matter of seconds. The boy reached me super fast. When he hugged me, I hugged him back and held him as tight and low as I could. I hugged this boy like I was his own father trying to save him from the end of the world. The thoughts running through my head were to save my guys. I was prepared to die for them in a moment's notice. So I hugged the boy with tears and waited for the inevitable. Except nothing happened. At first I thought it did and maybe my mind just freeze-framed the moment, but it didn't. I gathered my thoughts and look at the boy. He just wanted to hug an American because he thought we were cool.

When we weren't deployed, I had a couple different duties. Besides the everyday things like maintaining our weapons, I was also the soldier and eventually NCO in charge of training for Air Assault School. So I worked out a physical training plan and took the soldiers in my class to the Air Assault obstacle courses as well as taught them the things within the Air Assault handbook.

During my first deployment I was very nervous just from the stories told to me by soldiers in my unit who had deployed previously. I was also anxious during missions, anxious to know how I was going to react during a firefight. I became accustomed very quickly, and everything became reactionary. If we were being shot at or IEDs were going off, I was very calm, collected, and on point. I eventually started to enjoy it. The adrenaline high you feel during a firefight is something that I have tried to explain to people, but could never find the words. The only thing I could compare it to was love. It's exhilarating, scary, intense, and dangerous. But some people are built to run that way, and I always considered myself to be one of these people. Both deployments were very lucky for our unit in that there were injuries, but no fatalities. At first when I witnessed Iraqi casualties—whether terrorist or civilian—it was very jarring. After a while, it became like everything else. You just get used to it. It's a horrible thing to get used to, but that's part of the job. A carpenter smashes his thumb with a hammer. Soldiers must bear witness to atrocities. That was nothing out of the ordinary. It was just another Monday or Wednesday in Iraq.

I formed a lot of friendships during my time. That was something I was not used to because I only had a few friends growing up. This was a whole new world. You know that these guys would die for you. They would do anything for you, and that wasn't something I had with my local friends.

During my first deployment, there were phone centers. We had Internet, but it rarely worked. I would call home when I could, which was once or twice a month, mostly. Now by my second deployment, the Internet was a lot better and you could actually get it set up in your room during the deployment. Once that was set up, I started using Skype so I could call from my room instead of the phone and Internet cafes.

When I wasn't deployed, my friends and I were always doing something. I became very involved with boxing and mixed martial arts. I even got to where I was competing around the area. While deployed, if I wasn't on mission, my crew and I were usually at the gym. It was a good activity to keep your sanity while overseas. You work out as hard as you can and then by the end of the day, you're so exhausted that you just crash.

My family was overjoyed when I came home. They said it felt like they could finally breathe. The community was a different story. Not many of the people even knew that I had been deployed. I ran into some opposition a couple times. When I came home on leave from my second deployment, I ran into a difficult situation. When I got off the plane in Atlanta, I had to then rush to the other side of the airport to catch the flight to O'Hare. My friend that I was traveling with was going to New Jersey, so we had to split up. But before we did we ran into a couple of ignorant people that threw some very harsh words at us, with terms such as baby killer and things like that. They obviously didn't support the war, and that is their opinion and they are entitled to that. But they also didn't support the troops either and spat on us. That is a bit of a crushing blow to morale. Before you say horrible things to any soldier, try putting yourself in their shoes. Could you give your life for your country?

I've been out for a couple years now and I still have not adjusted. I read a quote that PTSD is your brain tuned to war, like a radio to your favorite station. Your brain is now set on that frequency and it's all but impossible to get it to change over. That best sums up my reentry to the civilian world.

I have several injuries now, and I don't sleep like I should. Little noises shoot me out of bed. I can't be around fireworks anymore, not even during the 4th of July. I have a hard time controlling my emotions at times. I don't like being in heavily populated areas anymore. I have a hard time even going to a grocery store if it is really busy. I can't tolerate the overwhelming amount of people on top of the fact I'm constantly looking over my shoulder. I am very hermit-like as of late.

I've kept in contact with some members of my unit, but I don't belong to any veteran organizations such as VFW or the American Legion.

Discipline is definitely a life lesson I learned from my military service, as well as identifying who your true friends are. I have pushed my body and mind to the edges of the world. From that I know that I am capable of great feats.

I have a lot of good memories from my service, particularly with my friends during our downtime. Boredom creates some very funny and interesting activities. The worst part of the war was the not knowing what was around the corner. My greatest fear was losing a member of my team or unit. I would have nightmares of something like that happening, and I would wake up in tears on a pool of sweat.

I don't regret serving my country, but when people thank me for my service, I wonder if it is really genuine or are they just saying thank you because they feel they have to.

Being part of this interview process for *VIETNAM & BEYOND* has awakened something inside of me. I wrote for years, but never considered myself a writer. I felt that I was lacking in talent, and that thought has stuck with me. I thought that the only thing I was good at was war and that guys like me don't become writers. But it's possible that war and fighting are not my only strengths, and this idea has revitalized me and is something I plan to explore.

Sgt. Robin R. Findlay
U.S. Army 101st Airborne Iraq
Illinois

"THE WALL".... a veteran's visit
From Thoughts, Memories and Tears

Names inscribed upon "THE WALL,"
Bring back memories of them all...
Fallen heroes, who were slain...
Their sacrifice, honored, beautifully plain....

Name after name, I see the flames...
Vast sea of black, I see the flak...
Row after row, the battle grows,
Ammo they need, the more they bleed....

Viet Nam, so far away,
All the soldiers in harm's way...
Thinking back, another day,
Jungle thick, so many sick,
How can it be? They're calling me....

Reflections of a bygone era,
Clear as a bell, as if a mirror...
Whistles blow, the enemy close,
It is night, one hell of a fight,
When it's done, we have won....

But what a cost, so many lost,
My friends, you see, all brothers to me...
I look around, the crowd has grown,
The names I see, so many I've known,
Heroes all, they held their own....

A young girl, she asks of me,
"Why oh why, how can this be?"...
"They gave their lives, that's plain to see,
They gave it for you, they gave it for me,
They gave it so all, all could be free"....

It's quiet now, but people weep,
A silent prayer, for soldiers who sleep...
God bless you all, who answered the call,
You silent heroes, of "THE WALL"...

Sleep in peace, your battles done,
Be it known, that you have won...
In the Kingdom of God, your life, will never end,
For it was you, who laid down his life, for his friends.

Peter S. Griffin
Company A, 2/502nd Infantry
101st Airborne Division
Vietnam 1965–66
Griffin's Lair: http://www.grifslair.com

Epilogue

The origins of writing this book have occurred like many things in my life. They weren't part of some master plan that had been thought out thoroughly many years in advance. To the contrary, I just kind of stumbled into it. To sum it up, I'd have to use a quote from John Lennon that my daughter had brought to my attention many years ago, "Life is what happens while you are busy making other plans". You can say that again.

Although my life has so far encompassed 66 years and in order not to go off on dozens of tangents, I'll try to focus on just a few parts and keep it short. I was not a "Wall Flower". I charged my share of windmills and crossed swords with the wrong Zorro.

My Father, David Markson served in World War One and my Uncle Joe, Uncle Ernie, Uncle Bill, Uncle Mickey and Uncle Frank, all served in World War Two. Uncle Joe Tengi, my mother's brother was killed while serving with the Third Armored Infantry Division of the First Army in Germany during March 1945. My service began with being stationed at Lackland Air Force Base in San Antonio, Texas for basic training and also for Air Police Technical School. I was then assigned to Portsmouth, New Hampshire a SAC (Strategic Air Command) base. S AC was the brainchild of the notorious World War Two

General, Curtis E. Lemay. From there I went to The Republic of South Vietnam March, 1967 to March, 1968 and then on to Holland, where I finished my enlistment

First and foremost and without this chain of events I never would have been able to write this book. I was a well hidden, double anchored, in deep denial, Vietnam Veteran. I almost even had myself convinced that I had never been there, that it had never happened. But it did. When Richie Spera passed on, it made me think. When Jackie Frasso took his life, it made me act. The time had come and ever so carefully I peered out of my well-insulated "emotional bunker" and sought out psychiatric help. That was in early 2007, only a few months after Jackie's death and 39 years after I had left Vietnam. Deep down inside me somewhere was a very sensitive, vulnerable place that I kept hidden and protected at all costs. I became an expert at "numbing". That "numbing" would overflow into other parts of my life. After two children and about 15 years, my marriage would end in divorce. At the time there wasn't even a diagnosis for PTSD. Things were going on but no one could put a finger on it. At a recent get together at my VFW, 4 of us, all Vietnam Vets, over a few beers realized that we had all been divorced. Was it a coincidence, maybe and then again maybe not? Initially I was assigned to a VA mental health caseworker, I attended weekly sessions. I would also see a psychologist and if I remember correctly she explained to me there were three things they explored during diagnosis.

How you were brought up, what you experienced in the War zone and what you experienced when you came home. Made sense to me. I continue to see the same mental health case worker at the VA that has seen me for the last seven years. I go approximately once every 4 or 5 weeks. I can discuss any and everything I need to. I didn't have to worry about what I said, because I was trying to get a job on the police department and they might think I'm crazy and disqualify me. So I tell it like it is. And most people don't really want to hear it. But where I go, it's safe and they do listen and they do want to hear it. From a recent update of my situation and at my request, my mental health caseworker wrote the following:

"Through harm reduction, this Veteran has been reducing the amount and frequency of drinking, yet he continues to suffer with intrusive memories, disturbed sleeping, exaggerated startle reaction, hyper vigilance, isolates to avoid conflict and is unable to control tears with traumatic reminders. This Veteran is occupationally and socially impaired with deficiencies in most areas. This condition is more likely than not related to Veteran's combat experiences endured during his service."

The Vietnam Protestors did what they believed in and so did I. I would like it to stay that way. I believe that was one of the reasons I went to Vietnam for in the first place. That is what sets Americans apart, the privilege to pursue your beliefs as you choose. I have no regrets going to Vietnam. But when people thank me for my service, I usually tear up. I get very emotional when people thank me for my service today, especially because there was no "thank you" to Vietnam Vets for decades. My Family reception when returning home was the best. The community gives me a bad feeling even when I think about it today.

Honorably discharged in May 1970, I did some wandering around before "Life happened to me". I had some money so I took one of those "On The Road" trips and drove, by myself, from New York to California, stopping off at the homes of a few Veteran friends who had told me to stop by if you are ever in so and so and I did. I took my Sister up on one of those employee discount airline tickets and headed for Tahiti. What a trip. I managed to spend almost a month in French Polynesia, visiting 5 islands and I even remember their names, Tahiti, Moorea, Bora Bora, Raiatea and an atoll known as Rangiroa. When I came back to Los Angeles where my Sister was living, I had $5.00 to my name. It was a great trip.

Back home now I continued to meander and didn't know what to do with myself. I had a dream about becoming a heavy equipment operator and eventually got into The Operating

Engineers Union, operating a front end loader and loading dump trucks in the South Florida area around Miami. Making good money, I was living the American Dream, back in the 70's when the dream still existed. But I had an itch I just couldn't scratch. I still wanted that Air Traffic Controllers job that had eluded me in the Air Force. I also had the G. I. bill which would pay for college and pay me too. I took advantage of it all and entered a cooperative education program in a local college and long story short got hired by The Federal Aviation Administration as an air traffic controller. Life got even better. But that would be short lived. On August 3rd, 1981 as a member of The Professional Air Traffic Controllers Organization, I walked off my job at New York City's LaGuardia airport and went on strike. We "crossed swords with the wrong Zorro". Forty Eight hours later Ronald Reagan would fire 15,000 of us and I was one of them. It was a blow I would never recover from professionally. It was and still is a one of a kind skill, that you either have or have not and I really loved the job. Sure, I made money and paid the bills, worked at jobs I was over qualified for, but I would never enjoy my profession or experience that special camaraderie of an Air Traffic Control Crew again, ever.

There has been much written about PTSD (Post Traumatic Stress Disorder), yet it remains a study in progress. All too often the media will cover a returning Veteran with open arms welcoming a son or a daughter at an airport. And at first glance it looks like "AAAhhh, what a happy ending", but the reality is turning out otherwise. The studies have already begun as to what happens to that happy family when the symptoms of the War zone start to manifest. War changes the soldier. It changes his family too. The psychiatric profession has already coined a term for it, Secondary PTSD. I take issue with the long-standing stoic credo, "We don't talk about it". What do we do then? Go out and get drunk and slam into a telephone pole going 90 miles an hour? Take life-threatening chances and crash into a tree on a snowmobile? Have an accidental discharge of a firearm? The suicide rate among Veterans has reached an epidemic rate, active duty and non-active is 22 a day. I'll repeat that; yes 22, every single day. This can possibly be avoided and I hope my message is clear. Some things take 50 years and this is one of them.

There were some great friendships made in Vietnam. When it came time to kick back and laugh at what we had been through, we laughed until we cried. However those friendships were short lived and unfortunately I have not stayed in contact with anyone other than a distant e-mail every few years. I don't understand why that is, it just is. I think of my two friends often, Jackie and Richie, especially when for one reason or another, I find myself outdoors in those early pre-dawn hours of the day and there is a stillness that sends my thoughts drifting back to those days of solitary guard duty on some remote post at Saigon Airport, in the darkness. I am and will remain eternally grateful for their service and for having them in my life.

When I left Vietnam in 1968 the possibility of returning for a visit one day was something I didn't think would ever enter my mind. However starting around 2006, I was over hearing other Vietnam Veterans telling stories of return trips. Around the same time I met a former South Vietnamese VNAF (Vietnam Air Force) Veteran. It turns out he was from Saigon and the last time he was in Vietnam, was 1975, he had been captured by the North Vietnamese and they were marching him north to a re-education camp. He told me he was going back too. And he did. Upon returning he told me I had nothing to worry about and that when I went to exchange Dollars for the Vietnamese Dong, I would need a wheelbarrow to carry it. He was right. The seed was planted. Initially I was supposed to go back with a friend, Tommy who had been back many times, however knee surgery prevented him from going. I went alone. Tommy would however arrange a very memorable part of my trip. Tom's father-in-law was Vietnamese. You guessed it. On one of his many return trips, Tom married a Vietnamese woman from Saigon. They live in Brooklyn. Tom's father-in-law was in the South Vietnamese Army during the War. Sometime after the North took over, Tom's father-in-law was sent to prison for being in the South Vietnamese Army. When he found out I was going back to Vietnam for a visit, he insisted on meeting me at the airport and taking me to my hotel. And he did. It was a moment I'll never forget. He spoke almost no English. But no words were necessary. I planned my trip to coincide with TET 2010. I wanted to see how this Old Vietnamese Holiday was supposed to be, unlike what I witnessed in 1968. In the 3 weeks I was there I ran into less than 10 Americans and only 3 former military. There was no animosity. When it would finally sink in that I was an American who had been there in 1967-68 and returned, I felt a feeling of respect that I did not feel in the States. They would just stare at me and say nothing. Tan Son Nhut airport was the same piece of real estate as it was in 1968, same runways however the perimeter was way more congested than when I was there. I lived the life, Saigon was booming and the Dollar was as strong as I ever experienced it. I enjoyed myself so much that I went back again in 2011 for TET with 2 other Vets and we all had the time of our lives and reminisce often about the trip, the people we met, places we visited. It was all good. To those of you who have been there, no matter what your opinion is, I highly recommend a return trip; plan to stay at least 3 weeks to give it time to sink in. You owe it to yourself. You don't need an itinerary; you'll make one up as you go.

The writing of this book has been an opportunity that has had an emotional sort of a cathartic affect on this author. I hope that other veterans and their families will feel the same after reading this book. It made me feel all the events, people, places and pets, good, bad or indifferent that touched me throughout my life in one way or another. Many times I was brought to tears, at other times filled with regret and grief, but overall a feeling of well being and inner peace.

I can never thank all of you enough, the living and the dead, for all you have given me.

Truly Yours,

Jim Markson

Jim Markson proudly poses with his WWI Veteran father, David Markson who became Commander of The American Legion, Bill Brown Post. Jim would later become Commander of the VFW Post 107.

Footnotes

1. Vietnam source updates:
   http://www.historyplace.com/unitedstates/vietnam/index-1965.html

2. Vietnam source updates:
   http://www.historyplace.com/unitedstates/vietnam/index-1965.html

3. Vietnam source updates:
   http://www.historyplace.com/unitedstates/vietnam/index-1965.html

4. Vietnam source updates:
   http://www.historyplace.com/unitedstates/vietnam/index-1965.html

5. Vietnam source updates:
   http://www.historyplace.com/unitedstates/vietnam/index-1965.html

6. Vietnam source updates:
   http://www.historyplace.com/unitedstates/vietnam/index-1965.html

7. Vietnam source updates:
   http://www.historyplace.com/unitedstates/vietnam/index-1965.html

8. Vietnam source updates:
   http://www.historyplace.com/unitedstates/vietnam/index-1965.html

9. Vietnam source updates:
   http://www.historyplace.com/unitedstates/vietnam/index-1965.html

10. Vietnam source updates:
    http://www.historyplace.com/unitedstates/vietnam/index-1965.html

11. Vietnam source updates:
    http://www.historyplace.com/unitedstates/vietnam/index-1965.html

CPSIA information can be obtained at www.ICGtesting.com
Printed in the USA
BVOW04*0530221014

371755BV00001B/9/P